Word of Life

Pray Now Prayers, Devotions, Blessings
and Reflections on How We Pray

Published on behalf of
THE CHURCH OF SCOTLAND
MISSION AND DISCIPLESHIP COUNCIL

SAINT ANDREW PRESS
Edinburgh

First published in 2017 by Saint Andrew Press
SAINT ANDREW PRESS
121 George Street
Edinburgh EH2 4YN

Second impression 2017

978 0 86153 977 2

Please note that the views expressed in 'Pray Now' are those
of the individual writer and not necessarily the official view of
the Church of Scotland, which can be laid down only by the
General Assembly.

British Library Cataloguing in Publication Data
A catalogue record for this book is available from the
British Library.

It is the publisher's policy to only use papers that are natural and
recyclable and that have been manufactured from timber grown in
renewable, properly managed forests. All of the manufacturing
processes of the papers are expected to conform to the
environmental regulations of the country of origin.

Typeset by Hugh Hillyard-Parker, Edinburgh
Printed and bound in the United Kingdom by CPI Group (UK) Ltd

Contents

Growing

Maturing

Later

Last Word

How We Pray

Preface

Words matter. Words communicate our reactions to life – their syllables convey our thoughts and emotions.

'The Word became flesh' is how John's Gospel introduces Jesus; God's word to the world is to become entwined with human life in the life of Jesus. *Pray Now: Word of Life* is a beautiful collection of prayers and meditations that weaves the life of God into human life and weaves human life into the life of God. The 52 chapters have been written by a wide group of writers from across the Church and are arranged around seasons and stages of life.

However, there are times when God's people struggle to know what to pray. Here the Church can help by offering encouragement hewn from the personal experience of one another. Eugene Peterson has pointed out that the Church has a key role to help people *'pray and learn to pray'*. A new feature in this edition of *Pray Now* is the 'How We Pray' section, which explores ways in which people pray in different circumstances and contexts. It is the way that each writer offers insights from personal experience that gives depth to their words.

The words of this book resonate with the smiles and laughter and tears and questions and hopes and frustrations that make up life. It's a book to keep close at hand.

REVD DAN CARMICHAEL
Vice-Convenor, Resourcing Worship

Using this Book

*[Jesus said] 'I have come that they may have life,
and have it abundantly.'*

~ John 10:10 ~

Jesus used words to draw people to the fullest possible
life. This is a book of words, but the intention of these
words is to draw readers to meet with God – the Living
Word. This is also a book about life. Its chapters are
rooted both in God the giver of life and in the everyday
life experience of God's people.

Word of Life is the theme of this edition of *Pray Now*.
Although the title links the book to The Church of
Scotland's 'Heart and Soul' celebration, this is a book for
people of all churches and none.

The book is in two sections: the first contains Scripture
readings, meditations and prayers, while the second
contains a series of articles on how to pray written from
a personal perspective by twelve different authors.

In the first section there are 52 chapters arranged under
seven headings that reflect different stages of life:

- Conception
- Birth
- Early
- Growing
- Maturing
- Later
- Last Word

The chapters are written by a broad range of writers, but the structure of each chapter is the same:

- Scripture verse that links to the chapter heading
- Meditation
- Morning Prayer
- Evening Prayer
- Two suggested Scripture readings
- Blessing

Use the book in the way that is most helpful to you. The 52 chapters mean that a different chapter can be focused on during each week of the year, offering a stimulus for worship or devotion over a seven-day span. However, the chapters can also be used in any order. Some of them reflect specific circumstances of life and could be used at specific times. The chapters can be used for individual prayer, for praying in a family, for praying with a friend, for praying in small groups, and for praying in a service of worship.

The words of each chapter have been written with great care, but there can be times when the words of others don't seem to speak to the situation of the moment. The prayers and meditations included here are not an end in themselves, but a springboard for prayer. Sometimes, the heading or a particular phrase will be enough to lead the reader into their own prayers, whether silent or spoken. A few blank pages have been left so that readers can note down their own prayers or record ways in which prayers have been answered.

The second section of the book contains twelve articles exploring 'How We Pray'. This is a new feature for the 2017 edition of *Pray Now*. Each of the twelve writers has contributed a personal reflection on how they are learning to pray in a particular circumstance of life. At the end of each article is a page left blank for notes. As these articles are read, each reader will bring their own experience and insights; these can be written down and added to the article and perhaps shared with others.

It is the hope of all those involved in preparing the words of this book that God will use them to help people pray in the midst of life now.

REVD DAN CARMICHAEL

For more information, the guide '*How to Pray*' can be found on the Church of Scotland website at www.churchofscotland. org.uk/worship or phone 0131 225 5722 and ask to be put through to the Mission and Discipleship Council.

CONCEPTION

Before I formed you in the womb I knew you,
and before you were born I consecrated you ...
~ Jeremiah 1:5 ~

Seed

... when I was being made in secret, intricately woven in the depths of the earth.

~ Psalm 139:15 ~

Meditation

A seed is a roadmap,
an itinerary,
a bundled up code,
the secret plans,
the coup de grâce,
the hinge on which everything rests.

And it rests

in darkness,
in slumber;
it rests
and waits.

A seed is life
compressed,
life
before light,
life that needs light
to open,
to live.

Morning Prayer

Each new life, each new venture
we bring before You now.

Each idea,
whether from new sparks
or old embers,
we bring them before You now.

Just as You knew us,
as we were being made in secret,

so You know the plans
now being made in secret,
of new things and new ventures.

Be with us throughout the day
as seeds fall and die,
breaking open,
bringing life.   AMEN

Evening Prayer

As the day draws to a close
we think of the seeds that have not burst into life,
the opportunities missed,
the losses we cannot ignore
and cannot redeem.

May, in time, we let go of these seeds
and release them into the soil,
the fertile ground of
new tomorrows
where it is only the end of the beginning.   AMEN

Scripture Readings

Psalm 139:13–16   *Fearfully and wonderfully made*
John 12:20–26   *If a grain dies it bears much fruit*

Blessing

Bless the seeds we find,
the seeds we gather,
the seeds we scatter,
as we wonder at the new shoots bursting forth.
AMEN

Beginning

Let the same mind be in you that was in Christ Jesus,
who, though He was in the form of God, did not regard
equality with God as something to be exploited,
but emptied Himself, taking the form of a slave,
being born in human likeness.

~ Philippians 2:5–7 ~

Meditation

When did it all begin? Life, faith, hope…
It began in the mind of God.

Before time as we know it began,
all that existed was God:
Father, Son and Holy Spirit, one God, one in being.
All things were created by the Father through the Son.
Everything was very good,
but our first parents disobeyed.
Sin entered our perfect world.

The Father loved the world so much that He sent His Son
to redeem the situation and to save sinners.
The Son did not count equality with God as something
to be exploited and so emptied himself.
Before there was a baby in a manger,
the eternal Son of God opted to take human flesh.

The story did not begin in Bethlehem;
He was conceived by the Holy Spirit in the womb of Mary.
The eternal Son became the Son of Man.

Morning Prayer

Father we praise You for our beginnings:
conceived and born into this wonderful world,
a world that displays Your craftsmanship,
a world where scientists open up the mysteries,
by thinking Your thoughts after You.

Father, we praise You for our spiritual beginnings,
for our baptism into the covenant people,
for our experience of the life of the Church,
for those who shared the story of Christ with us,
for new-found faith and the joy it brings,
for the assurance that we are made in Your image,
and for the meaning, purpose and significance this brings.

Father, we praise You above all for sending Your Son.
We thank You for His conception by the Holy Spirit,
for His wonderful, miraculous birth as a human being.
Grant that we might trust in Him.   AMEN

Evening Prayer

Lord, at the end of this day we worship You.
At the day's beginning we had our fears and anxieties,
but You were with us through it all.
At the day's beginning we had our hopes,
and some of those came to pass.

Lord, at the end of the day we are sorry for our sins,
our failures and our shortcomings.
We thank You for the promise of forgiveness
to those who confess sin and turn from it.
Grant us the grace of repentance
and the assurance of cleansing and renewal
by the Holy Spirit.

Lord, accept us in Christ Jesus.
Fill us with Your Holy Spirit.
Guide our paths.   AMEN

Scripture Readings

Philippians 2:1–11   *Born in human likeness*
John 3:1–16   *New birth and new life*

Blessing

May the grace of the Lord Jesus Christ,
the love of God and the fellowship of the
Holy Spirit be with you all.   AMEN

Question

'Let the day perish on which I was born,
and the night that said,
"A man-child is conceived."'

~ Job 3:3 ~

Meditation

Job, oh Job.
What to do with you?
You couldn't possibly have done anything to deserve
this, could you?
You've lost it all – money, children, love –
and now you are ridden with sores.
You say you have nothing.
Your friends hardly recognise you as they sit in silence.
You cannot see what good can come.

So you hurl your questions at God.
To your surprise, God hurls questions back
and invites you to take control.
You stand helpless in the face of human evil,
between the monsters of Behemoth and Leviathan.
And right there – you begin to see.
That from the very moment that you were conceived
God has loved you.
In your questioning – you eventually find your answer.

Morning Prayer

Let me take one step at a time
as I begin this new day.
Let the sunlight of Your love
break through on my life.
Through the loss, pain and anger
that I may question,
help me to have the patience
to find answer in You.   AMEN

Evening Prayer

It's never as easy as I thought it might be.
I still feel lost in my faults and failings.
For all that I have done,
and for all that I have failed to do,
forgive me Lord,
that I might begin again – tomorrow.
Help me to do Your will.   AMEN

Scripture Readings

Job 3   *Job laments his own conception
and very existence*

James 5:7–11   *The patience of saints*

Blessing

May every new day
be a new beginning,
in You Lord.

May we have the courage
to know ourselves
to be loved and forgiven.

May that forgiveness
give new conception
to opportunities of Your Kingdom.

May today and every day
be a blessing
in Your name.   AMEN

Herald

How beautiful upon the mountains
*   are the feet of the messenger who announces peace,*
who brings good news, who announces salvation,
*   who says to Zion, 'Your God reigns.'*

~ Isaiah 52:7 ~

Meditation

Listening, yet uncomprehending,
looking, yet not understanding,
stuck in the midst of hardships,
sometimes we cannot conceive differently.
Yet … a word so rare comes,
that voices exuberant expectation –
'Good News!' is heralded,
proclaimed aloud!

The messenger runs with excitement,
buoyant, jubilant, abounding in vitality;
joy overflows.
News of what God has decided,
a word that will transform,
conceive a whole new world of possibility
for all bound up, trapped, enslaved in exile.

The messenger runs
crying out 'Waken up! Waken up!'
Now is the time to make ready, to return home,
to shake off the dust of despair and sorrows,
of exile hardships that cling,
to put on new clothes and be free.

The messenger runs
announcing a summons to faith,
that we can rely upon God
in every circumstance –
announcing the invitation
to join the joyful procession,
freed to live a life unfettered.

Morning Prayer

Arise, my soul, arise this day.
Shake off all that clings like dust.
Loose the bonds that weigh upon me.
Clothe me with Your beauty and splendour.
Be my certainty in this day.
Show me what I have not been able to see
and fill me with joy.
Let me run with unfettered faith
as a messenger of comfort and hope to those I meet.
AMEN

Evening Prayer

God of comfort, of deliverance, of mercy.
Thank You for the people and places
I encountered in this day,
for awakening me to Your blessings.
I am thankful for the joys I have shared in,
for the people I have met,
for the moments that spoke of hope.

Thank You for those who were messengers to me,
reminders for me to trust and hope in You,
to conceive things beyond my limits,
confident that You reign in every circumstance.   AMEN

Scripture Readings

Isaiah 52:1–12   *Awake, awake ... depart, depart*
Luke 1:26–45   *The Annunciation*

Blessing

Hear the Father speak words of comfort.
Hear the Son speak words of hope.
Hear the Spirit speak words of peace.
Hear the Three declare, 'Your God reigns!'
over you.   AMEN

Fragile

The Lord is the stronghold of my life.

~ Psalm 27:1 ~

Meditation

FRAGILE

/fradʒʌɪl/ (adjective)

> *(of an object)*
> - easily broken or damaged
> - easily destroyed or threatened
>
> *(of a person)*
> - delicate and vulnerable

How am I defined?
A flimsy arrangement
of cells and self
hovering on the edge
of an unknown journey,
teetering on the rim
of dangerous adventure,
balanced on the cusp
of being me.

STRONGHOLD

/strɒŋhəʊld/ (noun)

> - a protected place
> - a place where belief is defended or upheld

As I linger on the threshold
of what I may be and become,
I know this delicate crossing-over
is a place where I am held
and hoped for
and handed over,
a new creation.
No need for explanation.

Morning Prayer

Lord God
whatever this day offers,
may I handle it with care.
Give me gentleness of step
to walk beside the fragile.
Give me courage of spirit
to protect the threatened.
Give me the wisdom and ways
to mend the broken.
Hand me over to Your world
in my weakness
that I may be strong for You.   AMEN

Evening Prayer

I am tired, Lord,
of hard work,
of little to do,
of endless chores,
of tasks undone,
of too much noise,
of too much silence.
Restore my feeble faith
with the promise of Your presence
tonight and tomorrow.   AMEN

Scripture Readings

Psalm 27:1–5   *The Lord is my salvation*
2 Corinthians 12:7*b*–10   *Paul's sufferings*

Blessing

The Lord of Hosts is on our side,
our safety is secure;
the God of Jacob is for us
a refuge strong and sure.   AMEN
(Psalm 46:11, *Scottish Psalter*)

Creation

Before I shaped you in the womb, I knew all about you.
~ Jeremiah 1:5 (*The Message*) ~

Meditation

We began our lives in the heart of God.
There is no warmer place,
no place where we are so loved,
no place where the hope for our future is so secure.

We journeyed from the heart and mind of God
through love (or lust) (or the meeting of egg and sperm
in more controlled conditions)
to nestle in the warmth of a womb.
By the tiniest fluttering,
we made ourselves known to those as yet unknown,
to an incomprehensible world.
We are the created.

We cannot create on our own – not anything,
but in the midst of His creativity
we find our own ways to be creative.
All we create is in some way connected to,
acquainted with,
His creation.

He alone creates.
Kind words from our lips that comfort others,
conceived in an instant or over years,
were warmed in the seedbed of His mind,
awaiting the moment of release,
the life-giving seed ruptured by His grace.

Morning Prayer

Lord, I awake this morning
longing to know myself better,
to understand what makes me 'tick'.
Your word reminds me that I am
no accident of genetics.

My very genesis flowed from Your heart of love.
Your purpose for my life, whatever my beginning,
is good.

By Your grace expose me to Your good will
and purpose for all You have created.
Bind me in all I do with those around me
whose lives have been true to Your will.
Loose me from all those influences that stifle creativity
that I may live in the abundance of life
that Your Son came to give.

Astound me with Your knowledge of me,
Your love and purpose for me,
that I may rise up with wings as eagles,
sure of Your love and purpose for my life.
For Your name's sake.   AMEN

Evening Prayer

The day You have given, Lord, is ended.
Unwinding my waking hours in the presence of Love,
disentangling the good from the enemy of the good,
I pause.

For words and acts that blessed, in the giving or receiving,
for compassionate companions,
I say thank You.
For hurtful words, given or received,
for grace resisted, ego indulged,
I pray, forgive and heal.   AMEN

Scripture Readings

Jeremiah 1:5   *Known in the womb*
Ephesians 2:10   *We are what God has made us*

Blessing

From light of day to dark of night,
to rest and dream
secure in the heart of God.   AMEN

BIRTH

Upon you I have leaned from my birth;
  it was You who took me from my mother's womb.

~ Psalm 71:6 ~

Breath

Jesus ... breathed on them and said to them,
'Receive the Holy Spirit.'

~ John 20:21, 22 ~

Meditation

Such was the reverence of God's people
for the name of God,
that when reading the Hebrew Scriptures aloud,
a rabbi would stop when he came to
the holy name
('Jehovah' in our Authorised Version,
correctly 'Yahweh').

Remaining silent,
he would take a deep breath through his mouth.
The nearest transcription of the sound of that
slow inhaling, and exhaling,
is
YAH-WEH, YAH-WEH.

With every breath we take, from birth to death,
we repeat God's holy name,
praying,
praying without ceasing.
YAH-WEH.

Morning Prayer

Come, Holy Spirit.
You hovered over the deep
at the beginning of time;
You came as a rushing wind
to the disciples at Pentecost.
You live in our hearts now,
and You breathe through our prayers,
when we don't know what to say.

Praise You, Lord God, for You have created us,
and given us life and breath.

You are the air we breathe, everywhere around us,
silent, invisible, and life giving.
Without You, Yahweh, we cannot survive,
we have no vision, no contentment, no enthusiasm.
Without You, Lord Christ, we can do nothing.

Breathe on us, breath of God.
Bring us back to life,
accepting Your forgiveness,
and enjoying Your peace.
As we breathe in Your Spirit,
may we then breathe out Your love.   AMEN

Evening Prayer

Christ be with me, Christ within me,
Christ behind me, Christ before me,
Christ beside me, Christ to win me,
Christ to comfort and restore me.
Christ beneath me, Christ above me,
Christ in quiet, Christ in danger,
Christ in hearts of all that love me,
Christ in mouth of friend and stranger.   AMEN

~ St Patrick's Breastplate ~

Scripture Readings

Genesis 2:4*b*–9   *God breathes the breath of life*
into Adam
John 20:19–23   *Jesus breathes the Holy Spirit*
into the disciples

Blessing

Lord, the more You bless us,
the more You use us;
the more You use us,
the more You bless us.
Bless the Lord, O my soul,
and all that is within me,
bless His holy name.   AMEN

Fear

'Do not be afraid.'

~ Luke 1:30,
and some 77 other times in Scripture ~

Meditation

Birth didn't scare me.
It was the talk of others' fears
that shook me.

I didn't think I was afraid.
Then I heard their stories –
grown men who work dark nights,
comforted by angels: 'Do not be afraid.'

I didn't think I was afraid.
Then he shared his dream – my beloved,
reassured by visions: 'Do not be afraid.'

I didn't think I was afraid.
Then they said: 'Do not return home.'

And now, I am afraid …

… I fear for this child and our lives,
on the run, uncertain, fleeing
from the recklessness of those
driven by fear and power, unprepared to trust,
unsure of their place in the world.

In these uncertain times
I choose to remember
that the fear of those
lost in reckless power
is overturned
by the magnitude of the love
our God has for us.

And so I return to my fearlessness,
and trust in the angels who said:
'Do not be afraid.'

Morning Prayer

May we this day
live with the fearlessness of Mary
and the courage of the shepherds,
who, in the face of their fears,
nevertheless trusted the angels
and followed their hearts' yearnings.
As we face our fears today and daily,
may we know the magnitude
of God's love.

May this love
spill out from our hearts
and transform all who
live in real fear for their lives
and their loved ones.

This we pray in the name of Jesus.   AMEN

Evening Prayer

Oh my soul,
as I turn to the night
to the dreams and the dark,
may I refill with hope and love,
and so turn again to the morning
renewed and inspired
to live in the love of You,
risen Jesus.   AMEN

Scripture Readings

Luke 1:30–33   *The angel Gabriel reassures Mary*
Acts 18:9   *Paul is given courage from the Lord*

Blessing

The blessing of the God of love
be on us and on all we love
today, and always.   AMEN

Cry

Jesus began to weep.

~ John 11:35 ~

Meditation

Mothering the Holy One
embracing infinite vulnerability,
in meditation,
Mary gazes into the Mystery,
the impenetrable darkness,
Eternity's eyes.

Exhausted,
sated with love,
she weeps at the suffering to come,
sees the end, the broken Christ,
where now He lies, crying.
She sheds the tears of a thousand, thousand mothers:
for parents who have lost a child;
for the stillborn, and loved still.

Crying for attention,
for His Mother's milk,
crying in hunger,
crying for the empty everywhere,
for the earth's neglected, abandoned;
creation's disfigurement.
In unshaped sounds,
speech-less,
Christ's cries
commingle with the One who,
mothering all,
suffers all.
In the cave, Love is born.

Morning Prayer

In morn's stillness,
darkness succumbs to the Sun's rising.

May Your light
shine in my darkness.
Free from strife or shattered,
touch and transfigure my soul
with Your luminous warmth.
Knowing that Jesus wept,
that in the tears of every child
are the tears of the Transcendent,
lift my soul this day;
let me listen for the silence,
the unvoiced vastness,
the Unborn,
present, illuming
the minutiae of each moment.   AMEN

Evening Prayer

Tiredness and tears,
disappointments and disgrace,
darkness welcomes weakness.
Calm me, O Lord.
Jesus, speak Your word of peace;
instill my soul with Your *shalom*.
In Christ, wisdom weeps;
resurrection follows death,
every death.

Calm me, O Lord;
sanctify my sleep.   AMEN

Scripture Readings

>   Luke 7:11–17   *A mother's tears*
>   John 11:17–44   *The tears of Jesus*

Blessing

>   May the Holy Three encircle me,
>   enclose me in eternity's embrace,
>   rest, refresh and restore me,
>   that, at one with the One,
>   I may serve in joy another day.   AMEN

Still

Gone is my glory,
and all that I had hoped for from the Lord.

~ Lamentations 3:18 ~

Meditation

A dream gone on waking.
A cry unheard.
Not even a chance to draw breath.
Dawn measured by its emptiness,
dusk by its silence.
A future chiselled by
would have been, could have been, should have been ...

Survival –
always an instinct
but never a guarantee.
And life goes on, apparently.
Well, somebody's does.

Everything was ready,
the visible gestation,
thought through and planned,
in hope and excitement,
so much looking forward,
oh so much looking forward.

Looking backward now,
closing the door, putting
those perfect preparations
out of sight,
though impossibly out of mind.

A sit-down strike in this no person's land.

It
was
not
meant

to be like this.

Morning Prayer

Dear God,
will You please sit with all
who ache over lifelessness today.
Parents holding children
who grow cold in their arms.
Midwives of imaginative ideas
that die for the lack of vision.
Labourers risking the building of projects
that lie unused while factions fight.
Dreamers nurturing aspirations to the point of fruition
stopped short by calamity.

God, You too know the pain of giving birth
only helplessly to witness death.
May I sit with Your grieving.
Then, show me what good things can yet be born today
and let me be Your midwife where I can.   AMEN

Evening Prayer

God, tell me honestly,
when have You planted seeds in me
that I myself choked?
Where have You been busy coaxing new life
that I came along and trampled?

How easily we uproot what was going to be born.
How amazing that so many of us make it,
so many ideas and dreams go all the way,
so many lives are lived to the full.

May it not take sorrow
to call out my joy at the life that I have
and all that You have yet to bring to birth.   AMEN

Scripture Readings

Lamentations 3:1–24   *Song from a grieving heart*
2 Samuel 18   *The loss of a son*

Blessing

> In the wilderness,
> in fierce and barren aloneness,
> in the paralysis of time standing still,
> in the bearing of the unbearable,
> may God be found faithful.   AMEN

PRAYER NOTES

Welcome

*I will pour my spirit on your descendants
and my blessing on your offspring.*

~ Isaiah 44:3 ~

Meditation

Let us not talk of hope
and all the dreams contained
in the moment of birth
of a child,
an idea,
a possibility.

Hope crosses fingers
and without any input from us ourselves
wants the best outcome.

Let us speak more with expectation –
for to expect something
means the possibility of it happening
is real.

So may we be real in the world:
really there,
really alive,
really working
towards welcoming the reign of God.

Morning Prayer

In the welcoming moment
of this new day
may I quicken to Your dreams
that unfold before me.

May I bend time
with expectation
that I might make real
the longing You have for me,
one possibility at a time,

and celebrate with the world
the gift I am.   AMEN

Evening Prayer

Where we have met
in expectation and wonder,
may I give You thanks, O God.

Where we have met
in questions and concern,
may I find peace, O God.

Where we have met
and new things unfolded,
may I give thanks, O God.

Where we have met
and found each other again,
may I rest in Your blessing.   AMEN

Scripture Readings

Isaiah 44:1–5   *God's blessing*
Genesis 1:1—2:4   *Birthing of Creation*

Blessing

May all your beginnings
awaken to the adventure
rekindled each day,
in every breath and word
that welcomes the world
with expectation
and wonder.   AMEN

Gift

Upon You I have leaned from my birth;
it was You who took me from my mother's womb.

~ Psalm 71:6 ~

Meditation

To know in silence I am not alone;
to find in darkness You are there;
to rest secure, even when things are hard;
to find refuge in the midst of everything …
I lean on You.

Yours is the gift of life,
the promise of gentle protection,
that in every trial or danger
You are there …
I lean on You.

You will hear my prayers.
You will feel my joy and sadness.
You will hold me close
like a newborn child.
And all before I know or understand …
I lean on You.

Before time,
after time,
in every time,
in this time …
I lean on You.

Morning Prayer

For the breaking of this new day, I am thankful.
For the rest of the night, I praise You.
This day,
whether I begin with tiredness or energy,
You are with me – just the same.

Eternal One, all time is in Your hands.
Help me to embrace the fullness of Your Spirit
as You breathe Your life in me once more.
Whatever this day may bring,
let me lean on You.

Help me to trust that
in Christ I am a new creation.
Let me live in that gift today.   AMEN

Evening Prayer

O God, You have given the greatest gift,
and it is in giving that we receive.
For the blessing of Christ
and the new birth received in Him,
I am thankful.

Help me to embrace
the surprises and challenges of this day,
accepting each experience as Your gift,
And labouring with its meaning.

Calm the storms within me this night,
that I may know Your rest and refuge.
Let me look forward to the new,
for tomorrow will come again ...
I lean on You.   AMEN

Scripture Readings

Psalm 71:1–6   *God's protection and help*
2 Corinthians 5:14–17   *New beginnings*

Blessing

From beginning to end,
from breath to life,
from heights to depths,
God ...
I lean on You.   AMEN

Celebrate

*'And get the fattened calf and kill it, and let us eat and
celebrate; for this son of mine was dead and is alive again;
he was lost and is found!' And they began to celebrate.*

~ Luke 15:23–24 ~

Meditation

'Let's celebrate!'
Impossible to say without a smile, inward or outward.
The response to an occasion of joy and gladness,
that calls out to be marked in a special way:
a significant wedding anniversary reached;
an important exam passed;
a job secured after long searching.
Or when someone thought forever lost
is home again, safe and sound.
As if reborn.

A new birth – a special time of rejoicing,
a safe arrival celebrated in rites and rituals,
in the varied customs of different cultures.
But the delight of parents, family, friends
is the same in every place.
Communal celebration,
the joy increased in the sharing,
a sign that we are made for one another.
And for God.

God wants to be in on our celebrations.
God knocks at our door,
reminding us that He is the source of life
in all its fullness.
To make God's praise our life's first priority,
is to find life's other joys enhanced.
In God there is more to celebrate
than we shall ever fathom.
Here is celebration that will have no end.
In His presence is fullness of joy.

Morning Prayer

Living God, as we awaken to a new day,
we pause to give this day to You.
Help us to embrace Your promise of new life,
to celebrate the amazing grace that gives a fresh start,
to let go all the baggage that will hold us back.

As a mother's heart fills with joy
as she gazes at her newborn child,
so Your heart bursts with delight
as You look on us, Your children.
Let our lives today be a celebration of Your praise.
Knowing that we, Your children, are immeasurably loved,
may Your love flow through us
to everyone who crosses our path this day.   AMEN

Evening Prayer

Loving God, as this day draws to a close,
we give it back to You, the source of every good gift,
with all its hopes and promises, its successes and failures.
Through all today's experiences,
the good and the not so good,
You have been faithful to us Your children.

Forgive us for opportunities missed;
for kind words that went unspoken;
for failing to celebrate Your kindness.
Thank You for Your forgiving love
that covers all our failings
and continues to make all things new.   AMEN

Scripture Readings

Psalm 150   *Praise the Lord!*
Luke 15:11–32   *The return of the prodigal son*

Blessing

May the God who delights in celebration
help us to find joy
in the new beginnings that this day offers.   AMEN

EARLY

He called a child, whom He put among them, and said,
'Truly I tell you, unless you change and become like
children, you will never enter the kingdom of heaven.'
~ Matthew 18:2–3 ~

Child

He called a child, whom He put among them, and said,
'Truly I tell you, unless you change and become like
children, you will never enter the kingdom of heaven.'

~ Matthew 18:2–3 ~

Meditation

Awake – and ready, before anyone else is
to live the day, to soak it up.
Eyes open – but in innocence and expectation,
ready to trust, ready to receive
whatever is given.

Unceasingly agile of movement and mind;
unnervingly fragile amongst humankind;
only feeling safe when never an arm's length away
from the larger hand so ready to hold, ready to hug,
still ready to lift a smaller hand to be held.

Seeing through a window not yet opaque with subtleties
nor dirty with habitual misjudgements.
Seen too through that window,
every feeling paraded on the face,
raw, unbridled, from little things to big,
not masked like the ones
who have learned to hide inside with age.

Morning Prayer

I'm ready to go, Father.
May I delight in the joy of the good things
I'm looking forward to today.
When I reach for Your hand in the things I'm scared of,
may Your grasp be swift, strong and tender.

Are we nearly there?
Is this the day that the thing I've been asking You for
comes to pass?
Have You a good thing to give me?
Something today that will make me smile at You?

Whatever You say today, I'll believe;
whatever You tell me to do, I'll do it;
whoever You sit me next to, I'll play with;
whenever You tell me, 'No', that will be that;
because I trust You, Father.   AMEN

Evening Prayer

Sometimes I'm not ready to go to bed –
the day has been so good.
I've had so much fun
and I want to stay awake with You for a bit.

Sometimes I'm not ready to go to bed –
what happened today made me so sad
and I need something nice and reassuring
before I can close my eyes in peace.
Will You sit with me awhile, Father?

The little things I enjoyed so much today,
I thank You for them.
The little things that upsct mc so much today,
I pray for Your comfort because only You understand.

Cover the cuts and bruises I felt today with a tender kiss
and let me take the treasures I've crafted today
to bed with me.   AMEN

Scripture Readings

Matthew 18:1–6   *Jesus makes a child an example*
Luke 11:1–13   *What to ask of 'Our Father'*

Blessing

May your mind be as curious,
your sense of injustice be as furious,
and your heart be as vulnerable as a child's.

May your eyes be as wide,
and your room for joy and hurt inside,
and your trust in God be as deep as a child's.
AMEN

Walk

*I have no greater joy than this, to hear that my children
are walking in the truth.*

~ 3 John 1:4 ~

Meditation

We walk by faith,
in faith,
for faith,
through faith,
with faith.

We move as we walk,
learn,
teach,
experience,
encounter.

Each step presumes firm ground underfoot.
Each journey can be planned, or random.
Each destination may be hoped for, or dreaded.

Our first steps are guided and protected,
finding where safety and danger lie.
As life begins, possibilities stretch out
into a limitless future where it seems,
though we have not travelled far,
we are somehow closer to the heart of God.

As we step onward, we confuse childlike with childish,
and forget the reality that we will
always remain Your children,
wherever we may walk.

Our paths become more complicated as we grow.
Routes are accompanied and unaccompanied.
We walk from cradle to grave,
overseen by God's kindness.
Guided, redirected, encouraged, until brought home.
To be with God.

Morning Prayer

Walking God,
be with us as we continue the journey of life
each day.
Be with us each step we take,
in brightness and darkness,
where the ground is sure or uneven.
We walk with faith, and hope, and love.
Let each step today be bathed in grace,
and illuminated by love.   AMEN

Evening Prayer

As day draws to its close,
we rest our weary feet
and recount where they have taken us today:
the uphill struggles,
the downhill coasting.
Lord, You have walked
ahead of us,
behind us,
beside us.
Our walking now complete this day,
be by our side as stillness falls over us.   AMEN

Scripture Readings

> Proverbs 12:28   *Walking God's pathway*
> 3 John 1:1–4   *Walking in the truth*

Blessing

> May the God of blessing
> bless each step you take,
> walking with you wherever you go,
> in joy, in sorrow,
> by day, by night,
> till journey's end is reached,
> and you are brought to safety and rest.   AMEN

Catch and Throw

'Cast the net to the right side of the boat'

~ John 21:6 ~

Meditation

A throwaway line.
But all the same
it caught us
unaware,
unsuspecting,
unprepared
for rich pickings.

A throwaway line.
And all the same
we hurled it skywards
with childish glee,
grabbed its rough edges,
plunged it deep
in practised resignation
and silent hope.

A throwaway line.
And nothing was the same
as we hauled it home,
sticky fingers grasping
at the glistening harvest
skittering and sparkling
among our feet.

A throwaway line
turned from net to wood,
and though we fumble
and are careless,
it catches us
and gathers us
and brings us home rejoicing.

Morning Prayer

Every day, everywhere
are glimpses of Your glory, Lord.
Creation basks in the warmth of the sun's rays
and I know that You hold me.
Clouds throw their cover over the earth
and I know that You enfold me.

Today, Lord God,
scatter Your grace around me
that I might haul it in
and marvel at its beauty.
And may I be ready to let it go
so others may catch sight of You.   AMEN

Evening Prayer

Spirit God,
who entered hearts
and tugged at souls,
untangle my thoughts
and smooth them out this night.
Make them ready
to trap the dreams
You throw my way.
And if some should slip
through the net,
then save them
for another time.   AMEN

Scripture Readings

John 21:1–9   *Jesus appears to the fishermen*
Acts 19:1–7   *Disciples receive the Holy Spirit*

Blessing

May God's love
grasp and clasp you
and God's Spirit
open your heart
to His keeping.   AMEN

Encourage/Discourage

'I will not fail you or forsake you.'

~ Joshua 1:5*c* ~

Meditation

Apprentice, acolyte, warrior, scout,
trained for leadership from early on
by Moses: this Joshua/Jesus* is all about
courage, faith, what resolve to carry on

obeying, the way God wanted things.
He needs every promise, all He can get
from a God who says He'll give wings
to His feet as He walks each day; yet

from Joshua to me is a long, long way
– like crossing the Jordan – Lord, show me
You're here right beside me, come what may;
lead me, follow me; after all, You know me.

**Jesus and Joshua are the Greek and Hebrew equivalents
of the same name.*

Morning Prayer

Lord, as this day begins, let me consider well
what You have said.
Your promise never to let me down.
Your promise never to let me go.
Encouraged, I take my stand upon these promises,
and seek firm ground for my feet today.

Lord, deliver me and others from discouragement.
I name these others before You now . . .
May we grow in faith, in hope, in love;
may we learn how to laugh at the devil;
may we discern through the bustle and noise of daily life
the growing shape of Your Kingdom,
through Jesus Christ.   AMEN

Evening Prayer

Tonight, Lord God, I name some of the things in the
world that discourage people of good will . . .
and some of the things
that are discouraging to me . . .
I will also name folk
who are burdened by many things like this . . .

Set scales before me.
On one side I will pile all these discouragements.
On the other I will place Your word,
and the hope of Your Kingdom.

Now, with the help of Your Spirit,
I shall see what has true weight and a real future.
I will think of Jesus,
who has overcome the powers of darkness,
and see things in His light,
I may even get a taste
of the powers of the world to come.
I will rejoice in the wonder of what lies ahead,
through Jesus Christ
who is the same yesterday,
today and for ever.   AMEN

Scripture readings

Joshua 1:1–9   *The Lord's encouragement to Joshua*
Acts 11:19–26   *Barnabas is sent to encourage the*
                church at Antioch

Blessing

May the Father who lifts the fallen set you upright,
   no longer ashamed.

May the Son who heals the outcast make you whole,
   no longer damaged.

May the Spirit who touches things of earth with flame
   fill your life with colour and joy.   AMEN

Baptism

'What must I do to be saved?'

~ Acts 16:30 ~

Meditation

May you hear the harmony
in flowing water
that flows with the promise
of renewal.

May you find the beauty
that cleanses you
from the stoor of the world
and the hurt of the past.

May you allow belonging
to invite you once more
onto the path of life
to travel in fellowship.

May you hear blessing
whispered and folded
around and within
God's generous life.

Morning Prayer

Regardless of age,
may my faith ever be renewed, O God,
within the promises You have set in me
and have invited me to uncover
over a lifetime of travelling.

May this day be yet another moment
where something old in me
touches something new in You
and grace baptises the present
with the curve of wisdom,
that invites me,
calls me,

longs for me
to see
anew
once more.   AMEN

Evening Prayer

What was new today
seems tireder now,
yet still it has been a gift
that has coloured and shaped me,
and I thank You, O God,
for the presence You have been
by grace
and with hope
through all things.

May this evening's end
be tomorrow's beginning,
renewed in the grace of the night
and reborn in the morning.   AMEN

Scripture Readings

Acts 16:25–34   *The jailer's baptism*
Galatians 3:23–29   *Clothed in Christ*

Blessing

May the Spirit enlighten you
through the promise of renewal
and baptise you with the light
that makes all things new.   AMEN

Lullaby

Pharaoh's daughter said to her, 'Yes.' So the girl went and called the child's mother. Pharaoh's daughter said to her, 'Take this child and nurse it for me, and I will give you your wages.' So the woman took the child and nursed it.

~ Exodus 2:8–9 ~

Meditation

The Moses basket sits by the bed,
a symbol of pregnant hope and excitement.
The anticipation of a first-born child,
a little baby girl,
to be welcomed and loved by all;
blankets and bedding, carefully chosen, lovingly picked;
dreams of lullabies and warm cuddles
when baby arrives.

She's been crying for an hour now,
but it feels like years,
little arms and legs
thrashing about in the basket,
replaced by rhythmic sobs and gulps of air
longing for comfort.

Her mother longs to comfort her,
soothe her with a lullaby.
She's all that she ever wanted,
a beautiful baby girl.

But there's no lullaby,
for the pain of depression
is just too much to bear.

Morning Prayer

Loving God,
more than Mother, more than Father,
we pray today for women who suffer from
post-natal depression.

Comfort them in their pain and confusion
as they battle with
conflicting feelings and disappointments.
Cradle them with Your love
that they may know that they and their babies
are loved more than they can ever imagine.   AMEN

Evening Prayer

Let us give thanks for those
who have received help this day;
for a comforting visit, a reassuring health visitor,
a signpost to help and a promise to be back.

Let us also pray for those
who have stumbled blindly in circles today,
where hope and help is a distant possibility;
for the unnoticed and forgotten,
and for those who can still put on a brave face.

Let us pray for wider families
who are affected by mental health issues.
Give all who struggle, courage and faith in themselves
to seek help and professional care.   AMEN

Scripture Readings

Psalm 139	*God is with us in the deepest valleys of despair*
Exodus 2	*The Birth of Moses*

Blessing

May you be blessed with the hope of
   a brighter tomorrow.
May God raise you up from the depths
   of your despair.
May sunshine chase away your fear
   and may you know the love of God
   this day and for evermore.   AMEN

Play

I was with Him as someone He could trust.
For me, every day was pure delight,
as I played in His presence all the time.

~ Proverbs 8:30 (*Complete Jewish Bible*) ~

Meditation

Wisdom plays as a child
beside God,
filled with wonder along the pathway of life.
Wide-eyed
to God's creative work.
There in the midst
found playing
she delights in God and creation.
An ode to joy!
Child's play with a whole world.

How we forget in our complex
adult living that we are called to be a child of God.
We disdain play;
we forget how to play;
we become passive spectators.
Yet playfulness makes us creative,
enlivens us and is formful in our lives.

Where is the delight as a result of play in my life?
Where is the playfulness in creativity,
the things that enliven life,
that help shape and form me as a person?

What does it mean in faith to play in God's presence
each day?

Morning Prayer

You created me to be Your child.
Like a child playing, delighting, learning, and growing.
Through this day
let me live in Your world,

to be awestruck,
to experience the joy of discovering afresh,
to enjoy and delight and play,
discerning the path You make
that is wise – righteous, just and fair.
Lead me through this day
on wisdom's playful path,
discovering and discerning
the wonders of the world around me.   AMEN

Evening Prayer

I am lost in wonder, love and praise.
Your craftsmanship,
leaves me wide-eyed,
full of wonder and awe.
Too much to grasp!
Overwhelmed to be a child of God
and that You delight in me.
Thankful for the vast playground
You have placed me in.
Growing up in Your presence,
learning what it is to be Your child.
Knowing the joy and delight of play.   AMEN

Scripture Readings

Proverbs 8:22–36   *A playful child*
Matthew 18:3–4   *Like this child*

Blessing

May the playfulness of God bless you,
the wonder of God fill you,
the discovery of God enliven you,
the word of God shape you,
as a child of God. AMEN

GROWING

*... speaking the truth in love, we must grow
up in every way into Him who is the head,
into Christ, from whom the whole body,
joined and knitted together by every ligament
with which it is equipped, as each part is
working properly, promotes the body's growth
in building itself up in love.*

~ Ephesians 4:14–16 ~

Shout

'What is my strength, that I should wait?'

~ Job 6:11 ~

Meditation

In youth we find ourselves shouting more,
sometimes from exuberance,
sometimes out of necessity.
We find ourselves going further,
physically and emotionally,
than we have ever gone before.
So we shout to be heard,
and to hear ourselves.

We want to maintain a connection,
the relationship we had when we were closer.
We raise our voices as our lives ripple further
and further outwards.
We shout, impatient at the distance we have created,
pushing away but reaching back.

The sober child serious about having fun is giving way
to the world-weary adult who has seen it all.
We shout to bridge that gap
between innocence and knowledge,
childhood and adulthood,
morning and night.

Morning Prayer

We shout to You our God.
We shout to release the pressure building up inside,
like teenagers unaware of our
newly elongated limbs,
we stumble around
confident and unsure,
committed and distracted,
assured and awkward.

Growing pains continue throughout our life
as our bodies and minds adapt and change,
yet we shout to You our God,
our constant,
who hears us
and always listens,
whether it's the day's first breath
or the night's last gasp,
however much we shout.   AMEN

Evening Prayer

We bring You this day,
the shrieks of joy,
the roars of anguish,
the yells of surprise,
the howls of loneliness,
the cries of recognition,
the bawls of despair,
the cheers of celebration,
and the quiet words that follow them.   AMEN

Scripture Readings

Job 6:11   *What is my strength ...*
Luke 17:11–19   *Healing the lepers*

Blessing

Bless our shouts for freedom,
our shouts of gratitude,
our shouts of welcome!   AMEN

Kiss

... righteousness and peace will kiss each other.

~ Psalm 85:10 ~

Meditation

The pressing and parting of lips,
the joining and pulling away of two.
Electricity running between two poles.
The platform we stand on,
between arriving and departing,
greeting and leaving,
meeting and parting,
past and future,
the now and not yet.

The touching place between then and now.
The first encounter
between who we were and who we are going to be,
between expectation and realisation,
between us and another.

A kiss does not fuse solid,
does not solder two things or two people together;
rather, it is a current
that allows energy to pass in-between.

If righteousness and peace kiss each other,
it is an intimate connection
requiring the crossing of only a short distance –
the live wire,
where the push and pull
between what is right and what is peaceful
is learned.

Morning Prayer

As our feet kiss the earth,
as our lips press together
to shape words and thoughts,
help us realise that it is in this tension,

in the push and pull,
that we grow and develop.
Help us to see that the right answer
can emerge between two things,
in the touching and parting.

A tentative offer of acceptance,
exposed and vulnerable,
open to rejection.
Protect us as we make ourselves vulnerable
to the kiss of another.   AMEN

Evening Prayer

The point of no return:
life is never the same before or after the kiss.
As we grow and learn, we decide what we accept
and what we reject,
what defines us and what restricts us.
Heal the kisses that have hurt us,
that betray us or betray how we feel,
and help us to kiss in friendship,
in love.

Help us bring together the parts of our lives
that we have kept separate.
Just as the first kiss is a headlong rush out of safety,
be with us as we step into the unknown
where we risk bringing different people,
and situations, together.
May we kiss well and boldly,
as when righteousness and peace kiss.   AMEN

Scripture Readings

Psalm 85   *Righteousness and peace kiss*
Luke 15:11–32   *The father kisses the prodigal son*

Blessing

May our day be full of kisses,
electrical charges of possibility,
where heaven and earth meet.   AMEN

Excluded

When they kept on questioning Him, He straightened up and said to them, 'Let anyone among you who is without sin be the first to throw a stone at her.'

~ John 8:7 ~

Meditation

'Eli, Eli, lema sabachthani?'
'My God, my God, why have You forsaken me?'
Tortured, dejected, shattered,
heart aching,
alone;
on the Cross
Yeshua's[1] yearning.
Authority's victim,
religion's reprobate,
by friends abandoned,
betrayed,
powerless in the face of power,
shamed,
humiliated,
tearful;
isolated.

Parable and paradox:
Eternity's exclusion.

On the Cross, half dead,
in the darkness of His soul,
Yeshua knelt alongside the woman
hemmed in,
'adulteress' and God-bearer;
He heard the Kabbalistic[2] cadences of children
crying *'Hosanna'*,
teeming the temple with holiness.

[1] *the Hebrew form of the name Jesus*
[2] *relating to the Jewish mystical tradition*

He met His friend, 'demoniac',
mentally fractured,
not in his right mind,
now at peace, at home in Yeshua.

Woman, child, man,
poor, rich,
bisexual, transgender, gay,
clever, less clever,
autistic, different,
religious, ethnic,
disabled,
single, divorced,
abused, abuser,
in Yeshua,
in me,
Yahweh's yearning.

Morning Prayer

Holy God,
Mystery immense, inscrutable,
coterminous with the curvature of space,
at one with the hundred billion neurons in my brain,
yet beyond matter and mind,
eternal,
inclusive of all that is,
enveloping every darkness,
the Sacred in whom no one is
excluded,
or ever could be.

Enthuse me, O Spirit,
rejuvenate me with joy.
Rested, may I rest in You,
naked, undefended,
now.   AMEN

Evening Prayer

I offer You, O God,
the pain of my exclusion,
a rawness, a memory
that never fades.

Comfort me, O Christ:
forbid that my cross entrap me
in snares of unkindness, intolerance,
hatred of others,
of self.

God of habitual hospitality,
grant me the grace to receive the love of Jesus,
to love others and self
wastefully.
Soak me in spiritual tranquility;
soundless spaciousness.   AMEN

Scripture Readings

Mark 5:1–20   *He lived among the tombs*
John 8:1–11   *In a crowd of men, Jesus stands*
                with a woman

Blessing

God of all,
all things shall be well.
Enkindle Your light within me;
sparkle in the dead of night,
in the dark depths.
Banish my sadness with Your bliss.   AMEN

PRAYER NOTES

Fire

When they had gone ashore, they saw a charcoal fire…

~ John 21:9 ~

Meditation

Fire brings heat;
fire brings light;
fire brings devastation;
fire brings cleansing;
fire brings renewal.

Disciples continuing in uncertainty
encounter Jesus by the lakeside.
He has prepared a charcoal fire
and on its intense heat a cooked breakfast
to nourish His friends after their hard labour.

The fire in this third resurrection encounter
attracted the disciples,
fed them, warmed them,
challenged them.
Fire revealed inconsistencies in belief
and their not-yet-mature faith.
Fire helped them see themselves as they were;
it illuminated Jesus too,
transforming darkening doubt
with firelight and His presence.

Morning Prayer

Spirit of God,
known to us through fire,
come to us this day to
brighten each dark moment.
May our fears be burned away.
May the warmth and welcome
of Your love comfort and console.
May the heat and passion of Your fire
purge from our thinking, speaking, doing,
all that is unworthy.

In the ups and downs of this day,
with its new challenges and unresolved issues,
when we speak without thinking,
think without kindness,
act without awareness,
purify us, burnish us,
mature us in spirited grace
that we may be fired up this day
to serve with brightness and warmth
our shining, nurturing Saviour.   AMEN

Evening Prayer

Within a coal the spark lies dormant,
waiting to be ignited,
so fire may come, with heat and light.
This night, let us lay down
over-heated words,
stifling thoughts,
and immature attitudes that scorched our interactions.
Within our sleeping bodies,
the spark of gentle, holy love rests
in the hours of darkness.
In the stillness of this evening hour,
we rest, but God's fire remains within,
awaiting the spark of the new day,
to reignite in hope and joy.   AMEN

Scripture Readings

> Exodus 3:1–6   *God's unquenchable fire*
> John 21:1–14   *God's resurrection fire*

Blessing

> The blessing of God's holy fire
> be in your thoughts,
> be in your words,
> be in your deeds,
> that brightness may be your example,
> and warmth be your love.   AMEN

Boundaries

You hem me in, behind and before,
and lay Your hand upon me.

~ Psalm 139:5 ~

Meditation

Security and protection,
limited access for others.

Pleasant and spacious places,
room to flourish and grow.

Scaffold and support,
opportunity to stretch.

Separation and individuality,
encouraged independence.

Confinement and restriction,
curiosity denied.

What of the boundaries of God?
Do they bring comfort or instil fear?

Hemmed in, behind and before.
Embraced and enfolded in love or
claustrophobic with no escape?

You lay Your hand upon me.
With blessing and healing or
with discipline and restraint?

Turning to the One hemmed in by the crowd
yet turning to see who had laid a hand on His hem.

We see her finally meet His gaze and watch them
cross the boundaries made rigid by law,
push back the boundaries made to exclude,
break down the boundaries of cultural hierarchy,
and redraw the boundaries of what it is to be hemmed in.

Morning Prayer

Thank You for the night behind us,
for the rest and restlessness it held.
Thank You for the day before us,
for the activity and stillness it holds.

And if there is more restlessness
or more stillness or more activity
than we would prefer,
hold us, God, so that by leaning on You
we find the strength we need.   AMEN

Evening Prayer

May we never tire
of crossing and pushing boundaries
that wrongfully isolate and exclude.

May we never tire
of drawing and fixing boundaries
that helpfully nurture and protect.

May we never tire
of extending the boundary of Your Kingdom
so there is more and more of heaven on earth.

Grant us the rest we need
so we may never tire to do Your will.   AMEN

Scripture Readings

> Psalm 139:1–6   *Confining boundaries*
> Luke 8:40–48   *Crossing boundaries*

Blessing

> May the presence of God
> hem you in, behind and before.
> May the hand of God
> restrain and release you to your fullest potential.
> May the wonder of God
> mesmerise and entice you to go beyond
> the boundaries of your comfort zone.   AMEN

Rumours

... they utter empty words, while their hearts gather mischief.

~ Psalm 41:6 ~

Meditation

Did you hear …
      … his parents weren't married?
Did you know ...
      … she was underage?
Had you heard …
      … they were hurried out of town?
Let me tell you …
      … he mixes with the wrong crowd
      … the abuser and abusive,
      … the criminal and crafty.

Rumours spin a web
that keep us from the truth,
only offering sight
of the clause that undermines.
Murmuring transfers
from external whispers,
to inner turmoil,
tearing at
the fragility of growth,
the awakening of self,
the belief and hope of all encompassing love.

Heaven's Gossip dispels mischief,
bringing together
the fragmented story
to reveal the presence of God
transforming human failing.

Morning Prayer

With creation's whisper,
You, the Maker,
awaken my heart this day.
The prattle of the Spirit
revives and encourages,
offering invitation to step out
into the unknown of all that lies ahead.
If the words of others wound,
be the balm that salves the pain.
When rumours stir,
lead me to the truth
that reveals the love of Christ
surrounding.   AMEN

Evening Prayer

Worn down by violent verbs
of foes and friends,
we seek a place of rest,
Passionate Comfort.
Within that space
spill justice and mercy
into our thoughts,
that rumours of the presence of heaven
disturb those we will meet tomorrow.   AMEN

Scripture Readings

> Psalm 41   *Seeking God's help and healing*
> James 3:1–10   *Taming the tongue*

Blessing

> Maker of Words, open my mouth;
> Rumour of Heaven, spill from my heart;
> Flurry of Noise, dismantle mischief
> with Your truth.   AMEN

Temple

*Do you not know that you are God's temple
and that God's Spirit dwells in you?*

~ 1 Corinthians 3:16 ~

Meditation

Searching for the body beautiful,
the stretch marks
of growing and changing shape
scar peach-like flesh.
Hormones rising create eruptions
that are treated with ointments
and covered with paint
for a more perfect mask
to be displayed.
Fabric hangings worn give hint
to the comfort of the temple
as baggy hides a multitude,
while form-fitting portrays every asset.

Hidden behind the decorated shell
the inner spirit searches for belonging
and acceptance.
Wanting to be loved,
this precious being must learn
to acknowledge love already offered
and rejoice in who they are.

Morning Prayer

With the Creator's eye,
may I see the beauty before me.
As the mirror and light highlight,
let me see the potential
not the imperfection;
the unique feature,
not the blemish.

In the eye of my Redeemer,
help me remember
that I am loved.   AMEN

Evening Prayer

The diminishing light of evening
casts shadows and dappled colours,
revealing an alternative vision of our frames.
We praise You for diverse perspectives
of those who have touched our lives.
Encourage us to rejoice in the qualities
others embrace and enjoy,
and that reveal Christ's presence at our heart.   AMEN

Scripture Readings

1 Corinthians 3:16–20 *The sacred nature of
human form*
Matthew 6:28–34 *Do not worry*

Blessing

Maker of our form,
bless the heart that speaks of love,
bless the mouth that declares truth,
bless the rippling dimple of the spirit's laughter,
bless the temple that houses Christ in life.
AMEN

Potential

' … out of his treasure what is new and what is old.'
~ Matthew 13:52 ~

Meditation

Treasure? Of course He meant
'out of the larder' in my culture,
but that is so rich – friends, family, experience,
wisdom growing in the school of hard knocks –
all that and my training in Kingdom life,
what a resource from behind me,
and new stuff in front of me.

No wonder Jesus spoke of seeds and leaven
to illustrate the mystery and promise of God's Kingdom.

No wonder He called young people to join Him
in learning to live for God.

No wonder older people would join the crowds
listening to Him, thinking about Him,
longing for His way to break through …

Morning Prayer

Father God, I praise You as I am this day,
shaped by what is past, open to the future.

Take the hidden riches of my earlier life,
spend them lavishly in the service of Your Kingdom.

Consider the unseen wealth of what is still to come,
invest it wisely in my life today and tomorrow,
and not in my life only, but also
in the lives of those I name before You …
in the lives of those who lead our public life …
in the lives of those who are giving up on life itself …

And hear the Kingdom prayer which I pray now
with all Your people: *Our Father in heaven …*
AMEN

Evening Prayer

Thank You, God, for the riches of this day,
for the wisdom of Your Word,
for the nourishing of Your Spirit.

Thank You, God,
for Your thoughtful presence with me,
which I am so slow to recognise.
Forgive me for what I have missed
or done amiss today.
Restore my faith and hope,
and lead me further
into Your good purpose for me,
through Jesus Christ.

Whether You grow Yourself, God,
is a question beyond me.
But I need to grow,
and I want to see Your realm grow,
in homes and workplaces,
in communities and dark places,
in hard situations which I bring to You now ...

Even as I sleep,
the seeds You have planted will be growing,
the bread You have yeasted will be shared
by people in every land.
Help me to know my place,
my potential, and my peace.   AMEN

Scripture Readings

Deuteronomy 11:22–28 *A promise, and a warning,
to the young nation of Israel*

Matthew 13:31–33, 44–52 *Parables of discovery, growth
and opportunity*

Blessing

May God unlock treasure for you from deep places;
may God unfold new aspects of His character;
may God undo any knots that hold you back;
may God unleash new power for good in your life;
may God uncover gifts to grow your faith and
fruitfulness;
and may the wonder of His Being
keep you steady in His service,
this night and always.   AMEN

PRAYER NOTES

Test

Who is wise and understanding among you?
Show by your good life that your works are done
with gentleness born of wisdom.

~ James 3:13 ~

Meditation

Where is wisdom to be found?
Is it just out there to be discovered,
or is it something to be learned?

From the earliest of days,
we are shaped in so many ways –
the tests and exams that have filled us with fear
have become stepping stones to here and now.

Sometimes tests are fun –
like taking part in a treasure hunt!
Other times,
they are significant hurdles to overcome.

Wisdom may say it is our attitude
that is the real test.

Let wisdom be God's gift.

Morning Prayer

Awaken me to Your presence,
O God, of all life.
Thank You for the gift of this day
where there are no mistakes – yet!

And when I find I falter,
as surely as I will,
let me know that I am held
In Your strength and wisdom,
and I can always begin again.

Examine me, O God,
and search my heart.
Find out if there is any offensive way in me,
and then lead me in Your everlasting way.   AMEN

Evening Prayer

The pages of another day have turned,
and before You, O God,
I examine my thoughts,
my actions and words this day.

You have shaped me by Your Word,
and given me gifts to use and share.
I offer You myself,
all that I am,
and look for You to help me grow
in Your wisdom day by day.

The blanket of night
often offers a time to reflect,
and I pray that You might find faithfulness.

Keep testing me, O God,
that I may live and grow in You,
and in your love and grace.   AMEN

Scripture Readings

James 3:13–18   *The wisdom test*
Psalm 139   *Growing in God*

Blessing

God in the testing,
God in the resting.
God in me,
And around me,
And I in God.   AMEN

MATURING

*... that you may be filled with the knowledge
of God's will in all spiritual wisdom and
understanding, so that you may lead lives
worthy of the Lord, fully pleasing to Him,
as you bear fruit in every good work and as
you grow in the knowledge of God.*

~ Colossians 1:9–10 ~

Branches

No branch can bear fruit by itself.

~ John 15:4 (NIV) ~

Meditation

With all the promise of a seed
and the exploration of the tap root
and the daring intuition of the first stalk;
through steady determination
and solid growth
of the bark encrusted trunk;
with the textures of wind
and run of rain
leaving their hidden rings;
from all of this
grows the branch
twisted by storm and sun
and the long experience
of a generation of wood.

Yet here,
at the newest edges,
where branch touches world
and light is absorbed,
is the place of invitation
to adventure further
into the world.

Morning Prayer

May I live today
with steady growth
and solid roots,
like the maturing tree
that speaks of Your steady love
that has always held me,
and of Your solid grace
that has always supported me.

Evening Prayer

Creating God,
in my maturing years,
may I look back at the twists and turns of life,
and recognise the broken branches,
and celebrate the newest leaves,
and in the daily rings that come with growth,
may I give thanks
for Your blessing of years.   AMEN

Scripture Readings

John 15:1–17   *Vine and branches*
Ezekiel 17:5–8   *Ezekiel's vision of the vine*

Blessing

Bless the air the branch encounters;
bless the light that feeds the tree;
bless the water that swells the fruit;
and bless the Creator who gifts it all.   AMEN

Politics

'Give back to Caesar what is Caesar's, and to God what is God's.'

~ Matthew 22:21 (NIV) ~

Meditation

*'I don't know which Bible people are reading
when they say that religion and politics don't mix,'*
said Desmond Tutu.

How we practise our faith and how we organise society
are intrinsically intertwined – as they have been ever
since we received the Ten Commandments.

Look at the life of Moses,
read the writings of the prophets,
ponder Mary's song of praise
when she hears she is to give birth to the Messiah.
And Jesus is crucified for being 'King of the Jews'.

In the parable of the last judgement the nations are asked
political questions, not religious ones.
To confess 'Jesus is Lord' (and therefore Caesar is not)
was a political statement as much as a religious one.

Politics can be used for good or ill,
but, we would have to admit,
so can religion.

Morning Prayer

Even Caesar belongs to You, Lord God Almighty.
Sometimes I give more attention to politics
than to prayer; and sometimes, I retreat into religion,
and ignore the realities of life.
I am grateful for the country I live in,
for all that it has given me.
I am even more grateful to You, Lord Jesus,
for what You have given me,
for what You have done for me.

For You are the Lord of heaven and earth,
and You are my God and King.
I long to see Your Kingdom come,
and Your will done on earth as it is in heaven.
Where justice flows like a stream through the land,
and righteousness like a river that never runs dry.
Where children are safe, the sick are made well.
Where all contribute to the common good.
Where nations are healed, and study war no more.
Where leaders are wise, and rulers compassionate.
When every knee shall bow, and every tongue confess,
that Jesus is Lord.   AMEN

Evening Prayer

As evening falls, Lord God,
I place into Your loving hands
all that has happened this day:
what I have heard in the news that disturbs me,
what I have heard from others that saddens me;
and all the things that give me hope.

As I reflect on my day, help me to see
where I have distanced myself from You
and where You have felt close;
and to discern what You want me to do with my gifts,
my money, and my time,
so that Your Spirit may work in me and through me,
to witness to Your peaceable Kingdom.   AMEN

Scripture Readings

    Isaiah 65:17–25   *Heaven on earth*
  Matthew 22:15–22   *The question about paying taxes*

Blessing

      Bless, loving God, our nation, and every nation;
      bless those who rejoice, and those who mourn;
      bless those whom I fail to love,
      bless my friends and bless my enemies,
      now and forever.   AMEN

Intimate

In the shadow of Your wings I sing for joy.

~ Psalm 63:7 ~

Meditation

There is no place apart from You.
Even in the secret places,
the intimate places,
You are there.

Do I always find that reassuring?
Or do I sometimes wish I could hide away?

But safe in the shadow of Your wings
there is peace and rest.
Your presence is not overbearing
but reassuring.

And as I grow to maturity in You,
I find confidence in life and faith.
You assure me that as You accept me,
so I can accept myself.

Morning Prayer

Loving God, this day I live in Your presence.
You have gone before me,
You are around me, and within me.
Knowing this fills me with strength and resolve,
as I look to be led by Your Spirit.

Speak to me in quiet whispers,
in gentle nudges,
in the meeting of friend and stranger.
Let the embrace of another
remind me of Your love this day.

I trust that when I fall down,
You will pick me up again
and set me on Your Way.

I trust in Your forgiveness,
and Your faithfulness.
Help me to follow in Christ's footsteps,
as I abide in Your love and care.   AMEN

Evening Prayer

O God, in whom I live and move and grow,
keep me rooted in You.
Help me each day and night
in the company of family and friends,
to find my home in You.

Stretch out in me the potential You see,
and help me to embrace the gifts You have given me.
Let my prayers reach out
and embrace those who need to know Your love.

I bless You God, in the wonder of the day
and in the watches of the night.
My life is complete in You.   AMEN

Scripture Readings

> Psalm 63   *Intimacy with God*
> John 15:1–11   *Abiding in God*

Blessing

> May the joy of knowing,
> the hope of believing,
> and the intimacy of sharing,
> keep me close to You.
> Always.   AMEN

Harvest

The fruit of the Spirit is ...

~ Galatians 5:22 ~

Meditation

An abundant harvest,
sign of favour?
A bumper crop,
a bigger barn,
time to expand,
extend to accommodate,
expand hopeful expectations,
satisfaction, contentment, rest;
the land produced,
this wealth earned,
all those years
grafting, cultivating, saving;
enjoy the reward.

Soul's ample goods
or a fool's treasure
for moth and rust?
Another kind of fool?
A fool full of divine wisdom?
A fruit fool of love, joy, kindness,
patience, generosity, faithfulness,
gentleness and self-control?
An abundant harvest,
gathered and shared,
blessed and blessing.

Morning Prayer

Thank You, God, for another day
ripe with potential.
Help us to pull down
any greed, selfishness or
arrogance we see in ourselves today
not giving space for it to grow.

Instead, help us to invest in,
store up and treasure Your wisdom;
to be generous towards others
and rich towards You.   AMEN

Evening Prayer

God of abundance,
back-sore but satisfied
we give thanks for the fruit
our lives gathered in,
shining with gratitude
and succulent with grace.

God of mercy,
weary with worry
we bring to You
the fruit of our lives
bruised with regret
and bitter with disappointment.

By Your Holy Spirit
touch, tend and heal,
transform our lives
to bear good fruit,
fruit that will last.   AMEN

Scripture Readings

Luke 12:13–21   *Whose harvest will it be?*
Galatians 5:22–23   *Fruit worth harvesting*

Blessing

May the wisdom of God,
the worth of the Word and
the treasure of the Holy Spirit
produce an abundant harvest
of good fruit in and through your life.   AMEN

Promise

When Jesus saw that [the scribe] answered wisely, He said to him, 'You are not far from the Kingdom of God!'

~ Mark 12:34 ~

Meditation

What did I see in You?
What did I hear from You that drew me?
Not only words
but Your way of speaking –
argument without arrogance;
correcting without condescending;
straight answers in the face of crooked questions.

What did You see in me?
What did You hear from me
that drew out that compelling claim –
'You are not far.'

I am not far?
How can I move closer?
How do I come nearer?

Keep drawing me, will You, Lord?
Draw out of me
what it is that You see.
There is something about You too
that has a pull on me
and seems so promising.

Morning Prayer

Jesus,
when I first got to know You,
what did I see?
Who was and is the man these portraits paint?
I sift again their sketches,
searching for what motivates You
and what You want me to get, now.

You were and are perceptive.
You like honest exchanges.
You don't mind being sized up
and You'll say it like it is in return.

You, who made no promises,
have kept Your word.
I, who promised You everything,
was deaf to Your chuckling.

How far? How near?
And what fond nickname do You give me
as You nudge and jolly me along?   AMEN

Evening Prayer

Looking back on today, Lord,
where was a promise made, kept, broken?
What did I fulfil of Your trust in me?
Who did I affirm or encourage?

You have a passion for the possible;
help me to share it!
You have a habit of renaming;
help me to develop it!
I want to love
with all my heart and strength and understanding;
help me to keep practising.

What was that, Lord?
I'm showing promise?
Thank You.   AMEN

Scripture Readings

Mark 12:28–34   *A mutual recognition*
John 1:35–42   *Seeing and staying*

Blessing

As day ends and night falls,
stay in the company of God
and of the angels –
companions, conspirators, cheerleaders.   AMEN

Voice

I have called you by name, you are mine.

~ Isaiah 43:1 ~

Meditation

Persistent gnawing,
urgent passion,
gently persuasive –
loud and clear.
The head looks for certainty and reason.
The heart loops and spins
as wisdom's energy plays
with the skill and talent of hand, eye and voice
searching for the perfect combination
of person, presence and place
to reveal Christ's prompting of the world.
Making a response and accepting the urge
can lead to a settled ledge on which to balance
as faith is revealed in the task of being ourselves.
No more pretence of ambitious searching,
instead acknowledging
the shape and purpose of God-given life and spirit.

Persistent gnawing,
urgent passion,
gently persuasive –
loud and clear.
The mind hopes for stability.
The spirit lurches,
chasing at the tails of the holy Wild Goose*
who senses the changing seasons of creation
and the need to take the gifts to a new height.
For while Christ's presence is unchanging,
our purpose and activity
must echo to the needs of the world
in which we are placed.

* *a term for the Holy Spirit used by the ancient Celts*

Persistent gnawing,
urgent passion,
gently persuasive –
loud and clear.

Morning Prayer

From wild dreams and whispered reminders
we have woken
to share this day with You,
all-embracing Presence.
Nudge us towards those moments
where the promise of heaven can spill into life.
Nestle us in the midst of people
who should be reminded of Christ's love.   AMEN

Evening Prayer

Internal Voice,
hush my heart and still my mind.
Settle me from all the tasks we've shared this day,
and let me gaze upon the wonder
of life shared in Your care.   AMEN

Scripture Readings

     Isaiah 43:1–7   *God's call and enabling presence*
  1 Samuel 3:1–19   *The call of the prophet Samuel*

Blessing

    May the Lord bless the choices I make this day,
    and inspire me to reveal all I know of Christ's love,
    whether I am full of energy,
    or sapped and drained.   AMEN

Yoke

Take my yoke upon you, and learn from me;
for I am gentle and humble in heart,
and you will find rest for your souls.

~ Matthew 11:29 ~

Meditation

Holding hands,
whispering love.
Moments of tenderness
that have moved beyond
the desperation of diagnosis.

Acceptance,
hands clasped,
sips of water,
tucks of sheet,
stroking of hair.

A final kiss,
a last breath.

***

She was my Mum;
I always thought I'd watch her grow old.

Through all of this she has supported me:
'You will graduate from your course' –
'You will know when you meet the one.'

From skinned knees to tearful break-ups,
her yoke was easy and my burden was light.
She had faith.
She taught me everything.

I've had to grow up quickly, too quickly.
I suppose that's part of this maturing process
we all go through –
just, some, sooner than others.

It was always just me and Mum.
Now it's just me,
and the faith that Mum gave me,
one prayer at a time.

Morning Prayer

So often we overcomplicate life;
search for hidden meaning;
ask for second opinions.
Very often the beauty is in the simplicity.
Help us to appreciate this in every moment of life,
not just when it all starts to come full circle.   AMEN

Evening Prayer

May we pray for those who care for the dying:
friends, partners, children, neighbours,
doctors, nurses, carers.
Grant them gentleness and understanding,
patience, empathy and kindness.   AMEN

Scripture Readings

Matthew 11:25–29   *Jesus thanks His Father*
Colossians 1:17   *God is in all things*

Blessing

May God grant to the living, grace;
to the departed, rest;
to the Church and the world, peace and concord;
and to us sinners, eternal life.   AMEN

Brokenness

Consider the work of God;
who can make straight what He has made crooked?

~ Ecclesiastes 7:13 ~

Meditation

Tikkun 'olam* –
to make straight, establish, arrange;
to repair the world that is broken.

The brokenness of Creation,
crooked and twisted,
deprived,
disordered.

The sheer brokenness of the human situation:
broken relationships,
broken dreams,
broken lives,
broken promises,
broken spirits,
broken hearts.

The struggle towards a vision of wholeness.
Yet impotent of making straight,
of repairing alone.

Consider the fragments of the brokenness.
The Restorer, Christ,
in whom all things hold together.
The repair in cruciform grace,
through the drama of love,
reconciling all things to Himself.
Tikkun 'olam

* *Hebrew for 'world repair', now used to connote social*
action and the pursuit of social justice

Morning Prayer

Lord, why the waste?
Your works of art
like artist paintings trashed,
layer upon layer
destroyed, dislocated,
fractured, shattered,
crooked, broken.

Amidst the abandonment, destruction,
devastation and ugliness in the world,
through the cross-shaped living of Your people,
Lord, make straight,
establish,
arrange,
repair the world that is broken,
restoring beauty,
as You reconcile all things to Yourself.   AMEN

Evening Prayer

In the quiet of the evening,
my prayer is hope-filled
trusting all shall be well,
repaired through Your Cross.

Even in me,
life beautifully bound with Your grace
through every trouble and sorrow,
every scar and broken part.
The crevices of my heart,
filled with Your words that make straight and repair.
Assured that all will be well through You.   AMEN

Scripture Readings

Ecclesiastes 7:13   *Reason for hope*
Colossians 1:15–23   *Reconciling all things*

Blessing

May today there be peace within.
May you trust God that you are exactly
where you are meant to be.
May you not forget the infinite possibilities
that are born of faith.
May you use those gifts that you have received,
and pass on the love that has been given to you.
May you be content knowing you are a child of God.
Let this presence settle into your bones, and allow
your soul the freedom to sing, dance, praise and love.
It is there for each and every one of us.

AMEN

~ Teresa of Avila ~

PRAYER NOTES

Hospitality

Do not neglect to show hospitality to strangers,
for by doing that some have entertained angels
without knowing it.

~ Hebrews 13:2 ~

Meditation

In the giving of hospitality:
welcome is extended,
gifts are shared,
inclusion is incarnate.
In the giving of hospitality:
there can be speech and silence,
food and drink,
shelter and healing.

Think of the times and places
when hospitality touched you:
the preparation and planning;
the working hands and feet;
and the kind hearts.

Hospitality can only work
if there is giving *and* receiving.
Is your giving and your receiving
open-hearted and open-handed?
Is your hospitality conditional or unconditional?
Were there times you had little to give,
but received much?
Are there times when you had much to give,
and did so with no expectation of return
because faith has led you to contented generosity?
Are there friends or strangers at your table?
Is there room for angels?

Morning Prayer

Lord,
for every table I sit at today,
the formal meal, the informal gathering,

where bread is broken
and thirst slaked,
make me grateful for all that is provided.
Hear my prayers for the providers:
the farmers, the hauliers, the shopkeepers,
the cooks, the servers, the clearers.
In the sharing, and giving, and receiving,
may Your Spirit flicker amongst those present,
that grace may abound,
and generosity be blessed.   AMEN

Evening Prayer

Where I have eaten my fill – my thanks.
Where I have quenched my thirst – my thanks.
Where I have been welcomed – my thanks.
Where I found a place at a table – my thanks.

For those who have gone hungry – my prayers.
For those who have gone thirsty – my prayers.
For those who have been unwelcome – my prayers.
For those who had no place at a table – my prayers.

Bind together my thanks and prayers this night,
that tomorrow, my faith may be informed by Your love,
and thoughts of hope may be turned
into deeds of generosity.   AMEN

Scripture Readings

Genesis 18:1–8   *Abraham's hospitality*
Hebrews 13:1–2   *Our hospitality to all*

Blessing

May the generosity of the giving God
meet your every need,
and inspire your every action,
that through giving and receiving,
you may share God's hospitable blessing.
AMEN

LATER

... even to your old age I am He,
*   even when you turn grey I will carry you.*
I have made, and I will bear;
*   I will carry and will save.*

~ Isaiah 46:4 ~

Season

He has made everything suitable for its time

~ Ecclesiastes 3:11 ~

Meditation

Add seasoning.
And spring awakened gently
nudging promises of growth
from dormant roots
pulsating beneath skin.

Add seasoning.
And summer gushed through limbs
like a burn in spate,
spreading and stretching
towards firth's release.

Add seasoning.
And autumn unfurls her warmth
to bodies comfortable
in their coat of wisdom
yet confident of fresh dreams.

Add seasoning.
And winter hovers around the bend
promising sparkling gifts
of memories made
and a Word kept.

Morning Prayer

Add something of Yourself
to this new day, Lord,
that I might sense Your presence
in the people I meet,
taste Your wisdom
in the words I speak
and bring flavour
to the work I do
in Your name.   AMEN

Evening Prayer

As sure as daylight turns to night,
as sure as stars pepper the sky,
as sure as years and youth pass
is Your love for us, Lord.

I offer You this day,
sweetened with thanksgiving
for Your great faithfulness,
timeless and unchanged.

I offer You myself
that I may be shaped and refined
for Your purpose tomorrow
and every day.   AMEN

Scripture Readings

Ecclesiastes 3:1–15   *A season for all things*
Matthew 24:30–35   *The signs of the coming of the Son of Man*

Blessing

The promise of new life,
the joy of God's light,
the warmth of God's love,
the freshness of God's grace
be with you.   AMEN

Reap

A harvest of righteousness is sown in peace for those who make peace.

~ James 3:18 ~

Meditation

What do I see on my screen today,
    perhaps from far away?

What do I see in the world outside today,
    but near at hand?

What do I see in my heart,
    close to me today, right inside?

Everyone is reaping today,
some in disquiet, some in delight;
some in anguish, some in joy;
what will they reap tomorrow?

I also am reaping, from seed I sowed long back.
And what will I reap when the great harvest comes?
I have learned the folly of boasting.
I am learning when to yield.
I will learn the value of peace.

In my life today and tomorrow I wish to make peace.

Morning Prayer

Others have sowed in many ways, God,
and I have reaped.
Thank You for all those
who have touched my life for good.
Thank You for those
whose harvest of art and science and learning
has been made available to me.
Thank You for those
who provide food for body and soul
that even today I shall eat with gratitude.
Thank You, God of seedtime and harvest.

Great God, set far from me envy and greed;
set before me humility, patience and love of mercy.
What I need for myself may I wish for others.
Let me desire peace, make peace, commend peace.

Evening Prayer

God of seedtime and harvest,
forgive us what we have sown amiss.
Nourish the good seed
that You have planted in our lives.
And when our harvest is laid out
bare or fair before You,
consider the One who sowed seed in human life
that will never rot,
the One who has reaped an eternal reward
for all of us,
even Jesus Christ our redeemer.

> *O Lord, support us all the day long*
> *of this troubled life,*
> *until the shadows lengthen*
> *and the evening comes*
> *and the busy world is hushed*
> *and the fever of life is over*
> *and our work done.*

> *Then in Your mercy grant us a safe lodging,*
> *a holy rest and peace at the last,*
> *through Jesus Christ our Lord.*   AMEN

> *~ adapted from a prayer by John Henry Newman ~*

Scripture Readings

| James 3:13–18 | *The peaceful seeds of heavenly wisdom produce a good harvest* |
| Luke 6:43–45 | *A good life, like a good tree, produces good fruit* |

Blessing

As your years, so may your faith last.

As your days, so may your strength be.

As your hours, so may your hope grow.

And when the glass is empty,
may you enter the fulness of joy
promised to all God's farm servants,
through Jesus Christ.   AMEN

PRAYER NOTES

Healing

He said to him, 'Go in peace.'

~ 2 Kings 5:19 ~

Meditation

Unnamed the girl speaks words that are testimony,
words that point to healing and reconciliation.
Naaman,
a foreigner, proud, an enemy,
afflicted by disease, stubborn,
rages at what seems ludicrous, stupidity,
a foolish waste of time.
Simple words from God's prophet:
'Wash and be clean.'
Echo.

Immersed. Humbled.
It was at a river that cleansing and healing came.
God's *shalom*.
A crossing over,
a being reconciled to God and the one who is 'other'.
These were waters that restored and made whole.

Who is it that speaks to you words in healing,
in reconciliation?
What are the simple words you need to hear
and immerse yourself in?
Hear the words: 'Go in peace.'
Echo.

Morning Prayer

At the beginning of this day,
grant me ears to hear and eyes to see.
Let me hear Your simple, clear words for me.
Cleanse me and renew me,
let the humility of Christ be seen in me.
Draw me, call me to the place of cleansing and healing.

Overwhelm me with Your *shalom*;
reveal to me throughout this day
those things in me and around me that need healed,
restored, reconciled, made whole.   AMEN

Evening Prayer

This night I lie down and rest
in the peace that You have brought me.
I trace the joys that have sought me in this day
and all that has made for healing.
Thankful for the things that have been restored,
for all that has breathed life,
for the opportunities to be reconciled.

I am not my own, but Yours, Lord.
Thankful for Your love that will not let me go,
I rest in You with humble hope.
I stay my heart upon You.   AMEN

Scripture readings

2 Kings 5:1–19   *A journey to wholeness*
Colossians 1:19–22   *Reconciled*

Blessing

The waters of *shalom*
wash over you
the grace of the Father,
the binding love of Christ,
the gentleness of the Holy Spirit.
May you go in peace.
AMEN

Resurrection

For since death came through a human being, the
resurrection of the dead has also come through a
human being; for as all die in Adam, so all will be
made alive in Christ

~ 1 Corinthians 15:21–22 ~

Meditation

The first man, Adam, brought death;
the second man, Christ, brought resurrection.

My inherited condition leads to death:
while still in Adam I am without hope.
I am not a sinner because I sin;
I sin because I am a sinner.

My new condition brings resurrection life:
now in Christ I have hope.
My resurrection life begins here and now;
I am no longer dead but alive.

'Everyone who lives and believes in me will never die' –
words of Jesus spoken to a grieving woman;
'Today you will be with me in Paradise' –
words of Jesus spoken to a dying thief.

I receive resurrection not because I deserve it;
I receive it only as a free gift.

Morning Prayer

Gracious God, in the trials and difficulties of this life
and in its uncertainty, help us look to Jesus;
Help us to see not only a man hanging on a cross,
but also a man who was raised from the dead.

Gracious God, You have told us
to focus our hearts and minds on things above,
where Christ is seated at Your right hand.
You have told us that we have been raised with Christ
and that our lives are now 'hidden with Christ in God'.

You have assured us that when He appears,
we shall be like Him,
for we shall see Him as He is.

Gracious God,
help us to hold on to these promises.
May these great truths of Scripture inspire us.
Help us to look up and not down.
Help us to find strength in Christ alone.   AMEN

Evening Prayer

Most loving God,
may the words of Jesus to the sisters of Lazarus
convince us that Jesus is resurrection and life.

Most loving God,
may the words of Jesus to a dying thief
convince us that we have hope of resurrection.

Eternal Father, at the end of the day may we:
give thanks for Your faithfulness,
give thanks for Your grace and mercy,
give thanks for encouragement and hope,
give thanks for the blessings of this life.

Draw near to us, as You have promised You would.
May we know Your life-giving presence.   AMEN

Scripture Readings

1 Corinthians 15:19–26   *Man of dust and Man of heaven*
Luke 23:32–43   *Resurrection and paradise*

Blessing

May grace, mercy and peace,
from God the Father,
the Son and the Holy Spirit,
rest upon and abide with you,
both now and for evermore.   AMEN

Remembered/Forgotten

Remember your creator in the days of your youth,
before the days of trouble come, and the years draw
near when you will say, 'I have no pleasure in them'.

~ Ecclesiastes 12:1 ~

Meditation

Remembered ...
Hearing and believing,
delighting in precious promises of
faithfulness and mercy.
A holy intimacy,
new-found joy
in the One who has known me from eternity,
whose purpose for me is good.
Is good.

Sharing with friends and family,
the bread, the wine – and the stories.
Sharing hymns and spiritual songs,
new songs.

How I delighted when they invited me
to join with them to worship.
Youthful days, fruitful days.
Days long gone.

Forgotten
This lonely reminiscing, casts a shadow.
I have forgotten the taste of the bread and the wine,
the voices of friends.
The harmony of the hymn escapes me.
I am forgetful. Am I forgotten?

O Lord make haste to help me.
And this I call to mind . . .
I remember,
I hear the voice of the One who is faithful.
I hear Him say:

'Can a mother forget the baby at her breast
and have no compassion on the child she has borne?
Though she may forget, I will not forget you!'
I remember His purpose for me is good.

Morning Prayer

This day, as every day, is Your gift to us, O Lord.
I choose to rejoice in this day;
in loneliness to remember Your presence is promised.
I choose to recall Your goodness
and the goodness of friends.
I choose to remember I am not forgotten;
I am held in the palm of Your hand.   AMEN

Evening Prayer

As the sun sets in the sky,
the light places become dim, shadowy,
veiling the beauty of the day.
Lord, You are present in the shadows …
in the shadows of the fading light,
in the shadows of my mind.
Shine Your light,
the light that testifies to Your love and faithfulness;
grant peaceful sleep to all who are troubled this evening.
AMEN

Scripture Readings

Ecclesiastes 12:1   *Remember your creator*
Isaiah 46:4   *I will carry you when you are old*

Blessing

Remembering God's faithfulness and love
accept His embrace.
You are engraved on the palms of His hands.
He holds and protects you in all situations,
always.   AMEN

Presence

Let your garments always be white;
do not let oil be lacking on your head.

~ Ecclesiastes 9:8 ~

Meditation
Life.
What a bundle of mystery
and ambiguity and contradiction.
Recounting the countless,
the stars and sandgrains of passing years,
beautiful and breathtaking moments,
mundane and mediocre,
arbitrary and agonising,
small and simple,
how do they matter?
Not for following patterns
or fitting rules.
Not for being systematic
or making sense.
Moments matter for being,
being lived and breathed in,
being the present,
gifted, received,
savoured, surrendered.

In all its vanity,
all its fullness …
Life.

Morning Prayer
God,
here I am
and here You are
in this sacred,
ordinary,
unrepeatable moment.

You know how it is in my heart.
You behold me with love and delight.
Today, help me to call to mind often
that I walk in Your presence.
Let Your spirit break through my consciousness
and keep me open towards those I'm going to meet.
Surprise me with a fresh and deep awareness
of how precious it is to be alive
and to be human
and to be Yours.   AMEN

Evening Prayer

God of life,
how has today been lived
by all Your beloved people?
Please will You come near –
soothe Your struggling ones,
hear Your puzzling ones,
soften Your sceptical ones,
pacify Your overthinking ones,
lift up Your defeated ones,
understand Your questioning ones,
embrace Your bewildered ones,
accompany Your contemplative ones.
And all for Your love's sake.   AMEN

Scripture Readings

Ecclesiastes 9   *Enjoy life for its own sake*
Philippians 4   *Content in every circumstance*

Blessing

May we go,
eat our bread with enjoyment,
and drink our wine with a merry heart;
for God has long ago approved of what we do.
And the oil of God's blessing
be always on our heads.   AMEN

Wine

When I became an adult, I put away childish things.
~ 1 Corinthians 13:11 ~

Meditation

With all the subtle layers
and experience
of flavour and aroma
formed from days of sunshine
and seasons of rain;
of warm nights
before winter chill;
of pruning and grafting
and summer tending;
before autumn harvest ...
The vintner's hand
has shaped
a lifelong investment
in the fruit of our labours
and such nurtured experience
that severely prunes
and opens the light.
We grow into a wine
full bodied
and richly mature:
God's generous gift
of three score years and ten.

Morning Prayer

In this morning light
may I be ready to grasp the experiences,
good and bad,
comfortable and challenging,
twisted and beautiful,
that this day brings
in a measure enough
with which I can cope

that I might continue to grow
maturing in faith –
but not enough
to let You go.   AMEN

Evening Prayer

May I remember this day, O God,
for the thing that happened
that I cannot yet name
or do not understand
but has taught me
influenced me
honed me
challenged me
forgiven me
and loved me
enough
to grow a little
and laid yet another layer
through the rich wine of life
I am becoming.   AMEN

Scripture Readings

1 Corinthians 13:9–13   *When I became an adult*
Luke 8:11–15   *Bearing fruit with patient
endurance*

Blessing

May life give you
a plethora of experience
to excite the flavours
that make you, you.   AMEN

Whisper

What I say to you in the dark, tell in the light; and what you hear whispered, proclaim from the housetops.

~ Matthew 10:27 ~

Meditation

And I have learned to listen
for the whisper of shells
    under the roar of waves;
for the shuffle of a vole
    beneath the leaves;
for the flutter of a breath
    nested in the clamour of the crowd;
for the stillness in my heart
    overcome by need.

And in the listening,
I now know the power of that
stillness, flutter,
whisper
at the heart of heat:
this is the power of our God
greater than all that can be;
smaller than all that is.

And this I have come to know:
to trust the whisper –
to raise my voice,
and to raise it quietly.

So let us raise up our voices:
for all wronged;
with the silenced;
where there is fear;
in the face of injustice.

And in this raising up,
let us stay soft
– whisper even –
and so be heard.

Morning Prayer

On this morning dear Lord,
I pray for the courage to
speak up and speak out
for all who are silenced.

I pray for the insight to know
when a whisper from You
is a nudge to make a difference.

And I pray for the wisdom to discern
those flutters,
whispers of the heart
that are Your voice calling me,
now and always.   AMEN

Evening Prayer

Loving Lord,
thank You for the day –
for all the good that has been done
quietly,
and for all the wisdom that has been shared
boldly.

May we know
the gentle flutter
or the raucous roar
that is Your Holy Spirit nudging us
to be bold, speak truth, have no fear.   AMEN

Scripture Readings

Matthew 10:26–27   *Be bold, speak truth, have no fear*
1 Kings 19:11–12   *The sound of sheer silence*

Blessing

May the blessing of the God
who whispers 'I love you' and
who shouts 'Be bold!'
dwell in our hearts and our hands
now and always.   AMEN

Stories

*'Keep these words that I am commanding you today
in your heart.'*

~ Deuteronomy 6:6 ~

Meditation

In an upper room,
darkness encroaching,
the disciple whom Jesus loved especially
laid his head upon Him, resting;
he asked, 'Where are You?'

'With Nicodemus. I remember
how I felt that first night:
the Spirit was afire within me
and between us; raged uncontrollably.
We were so alive.'

'Only Nicodemus?'

'I can still feel My feet being washed:
her tears, her hair, her gentle kiss.
And the ointment. I remember the
love. Sinful? Her face shone
brighter than that of Moses.'

'And I was thinking of My Mother
and what tomorrow will bring;
the burdens she has carried,
the love she has shared,
the wisdom she instilled in My soul.'

Feelings and faces flood the mind,
stories bestow meaning upon place,
space is made sacred by
love and hurt and joy and loss.

Jesus, amidst the myriad of stories in my life,
You are my story's central character,
the One who swells my heart,
has shaped and shapes all.

Morning Prayer

Holy God, the Sun's rising,
a testament to resurrection,
born anew in me,
may Your Spirit's warmth and light
raise my soul,
invigorate my faith,
energise my dealings,
that, with a wonder-filled heart,
I may hold on to the miraculous in the mundane,
the sacred transfiguring the secular.

The wind blows where it will;
blow afresh through me.
Today, share with me the birthing of new memories,
stories of encounters unplanned.   AMEN

Evening Prayer

Holy God,
I pray for those with whom I shared my life this day,
giving thanks for the kindnesses found,
the companionship and creativity.
Take from my hands
all hurts, disappointments and insecurities.
Grant me peace, O Lord,
strength, discernment and understanding.
Bless my sleeping and the stories of the night.   AMEN

Scripture Readings

Deuteronomy 6:4–9   *Keep these words in your heart*
John 13:1–30   *Jesus kneels at His disciples' feet*

Blessing

Encircle me, Lord;
protect me from all harm.
Hold me in the hollow of Your hand,
that I may rise tomorrow
renewed, born again, refreshed,
and emboldened by my eternal worth.   AMEN

LAST WORD

Then I saw a new heaven and a new earth;
for the first heaven and the first earth had passed away.

~ Revelation 21:1 ~

End

'I am about to be gathered to my people.'

~ Genesis 49:29 ~

Meditation

Jacob's life had its full share of bad behaviour,
suffering and regret, but he had a good death,
the kind perhaps we all covet and only some enjoy.
How can I trace God's providence in my life?

Jacob expected to be buried with his people –
a privilege some get and many don't.
How do I reflect on my likely funeral arrangements?
Will these be good for my family as well as myself?

John Bunyan said, *'If a man would live well,
let him fetch his last day to him, and make it always
his company-keeper.'** How shall I 'live well' today?
And how shall I pray for others, and for the world I
live in, that people may genuinely enjoy a better life?

**John Bunyan,* Pilgrim's Progress, *1678*

Morning Prayer

Dear Lord,
today I look back with great thankfulness,
wondering at the way You have come into my life,
picked me up, dusted me down,
spoken forgiveness and healing,
set my feet upon the path of life,
not once but many times.
For Your patience and persistence with me,
I bless Your holy name.

And I look forward to the days I have left,
whether few or many.
I do not know the time of my departure;
I may not know the place of my resurrection.

But I know the One in whom I have believed,
Your Son Jesus Christ.
I am persuaded that He is able to keep safe hold
of that which I commit afresh to His care.   AMEN

Evening Prayer

What a fragile world I inhabit, Creator God!
How uncertain are human plans and projects!
How quickly valued ways and treasured friends
come to their end!

Help me tonight to see all my affairs in the light of
eternity – and to see eternity in the light You have so
wonderfully provided in the person of Jesus Christ,
in His birth, His life, His death, His resurrection.

With all Your people on earth
I dare to look forward to the end,
knowing that death and rebirth
are part of Your purpose which touches all nature,
and has been sealed to me in baptism.

May God the Father sort out what is behind me,
May God the Son make clear what is before me,
May God the Spirit touch my here and now.   AMEN

Scripture Readings

Genesis 49:29–33	*Jacob's last words and death*
2 Peter 3:8–13	*A warning about 'the end of all things', at a time unexpected*

Blessing

God be in my head, and in my understanding;
God be in mine eyes, and in my looking;
God be in my mouth, and in my speaking;
God be in my heart, and in my thinking;
God be at mine end, and at my departing.   AMEN

~ from Sarum Primer, 1558 ~

Heaven

Then I saw a new heaven and a new earth; for the first heaven and the first earth had passed away.

~ Revelation 21:1 ~

Meditation

'Heaven is wonderful, but it's not the end of the world.'
Whoever said that gave expression to
an often overlooked truth.
'Going to heaven when you die'
– is that really the end point of it all?
Why do we think of heaven as distant, an ethereal realm
of wraith-like beings and celestial harpists?

Heaven is God's dimension of present reality,
our *post-mortem* staging post,
a wonderful place of rest
en route to a world made fully new.

In John's vision, the new Jerusalem
comes down from heaven to earth;
God's dwelling is among His people;
perfect *shalom* – the aim of creation from the outset –
has been achieved
as God and His unique image-bearers
share the same glorious reality.
After all, in God's plan,
heaven and earth were always meant to belong together.

Morning Prayer

We thank You, Lord, for our creation
and our new creation in Christ.
Today, let the big vision of Your fully-come Kingdom
of justice, love and peace
inspire all we think, say and do.

May this future of glory come to transform our present,
the people we meet, the tasks we do,
the opportunities we encounter, the meals we share.

May Your new creation be seen in us
and may we be its hope-filled agents,
living signs of the glory that is yet to be.

Sharpen our senses to all that points to Your coming reign,
in people, in ourselves,
in the majesty and beauty of the natural order.
Help us clearly to show Jesus to others
so that His sovereign, gentle, loving rule
may be joyfully embraced.   AMEN

Evening Prayer

God, we thank You for everything today that spoke to us
of new creation and rekindled the great hope
that Your will *shall* be done on earth, as it is in heaven.
Forgive us for every way in which today
we chose the stale and futile in place of
the fresh and meaningful realities of the coming age.

As the day draws to a close,
we thank You for Your never-ending love,
and for a future as bright as Your promises.
Be with us as we sleep and when one day we sleep in death,
may we rest and wait in the heaven of Your presence
and at our Saviour's coming, rise to find our place
in the new Jerusalem, to serve forever
in the temple of a renewed universe.   AMEN

Scripture Readings

Isaiah 11:1–9   *God's peaceful Kingdom*
Revelation 21:1–5*a*, 22–27   *All things new!*

Blessing

May the God who has promised to show wonders
to those who wait for Him,
fill us with joy and peace in believing
and by His Spirit empower us to serve in hope
for the building of His Kingdom of justice,
love and peace, until the perfect day breaks
and the shadows flee away.   AMEN

Paradise

When I look at Your heavens, the work of Your fingers,
the moon and the stars that You have established;
what are human beings that You are mindful of them,
mortals that You care for them?

~ Psalm 8:3–4 ~

Meditation

Paradise is not lost;
it is here –
not in the sense of perfection
or completion
or heavenly realms.

Paradise is here,
for we have harmony in God,
and in God we have life
even now.

Pictures of paradise are not real;
what is real is here and now.
I am loved and cared for
by the One who is Eternal.

God is my dignity and my delight.

Morning Prayer

Awaken me, O God, to Your presence.
Let me know You close
in the rhythms of life and breath.
You have already walked the path I will take this day,
and I am held and known by You.

I praise You God,
that You consider Your creation a means of blessing;
that You have given to each and to all
a place and a purpose.

Let me wonder at Your creation
and my place within it,

that I may live to Your praise and glory.
O Lord, our Lord,
how majestic is Your name in all the earth.   AMEN

Evening Prayer

God of grace,
sometimes I struggle in the passing of a day
to discern Your presence.

It is one thing to know Your promises
and to believe in them –
it is another to feel You near.

I know I have made mistakes today –
I have not acted always
in the way that honours You.
I seek Your forgiveness and restoration this night.

Remind me,
that though everything is not always clear,
that doubt and faith are healthy companions.

Help me to know more fully
Your love and peace,
trusting that I am fully known by You.

May my life reflect the life of Christ,
even in part,
each day and each night.   AMEN

Scripture Readings

         Psalm 8   *Majesty and dignity*
1 Corinthians 13:8–13   *Seeing face to face*

Blessing

         Let faith, hope and love abide –
         let them abide in me.
         May I be blessed by You,
         and become a blessing in You.   AMEN

Rest

Return, O my soul, to your rest,
for the Lord has dealt bountifully with you.

~ Psalm 116:7 ~

Meditation

In our busy-ness, it is a skill to find rest.
Rest that is not just doing nothing.
Rest – a life giver,
a pivot, a requirement of faith, a joy.

Rest that appreciates what I have been able to achieve
and restores in me my desire to be creative
like my Creator.

Rest that creates a spaciousness,
restoration of possibilities of new beginnings,
like a deep extended breath.

Rest that receives my troubles and complaints
and renews me, giving back a rhythm to life,
a zest for living.

Rest, any moment,
every day, every month, every year,
our heritage, like a beating heart
brings us life …

Rest that we practise, every Sabbath,
letting go into the unknown,
practising doing nothing, just being.

Rest, a step towards our physical ending;
preparing – releasing – being accepted – just as I am,
resting in life beyond death.

May I treasure rest and rest in the Mystery
who can transform me
to a greater image of love.

Morning Prayer

May I live this day from a place of rest,
a body renewed.

May I enter this day
knowing I am loved
trusting that within me I am resourced
by the One who made me,
who will never let me go.

Keep me returning ...
to the Source of life and strength.   AMEN

Evening Prayer

Sweep my heart clean, O Lover of my soul,
hear what trauchles and troubles me,
what weighs me down and leaves me dispirited.

Listen as I reflect on the life-giving moments of this day
and help me treasure them.
Enable me to let go of that which did not serve me,
or You.

Let me place all things in the palms of Your hands
in quiet dependence,
trusting that in the dark of the night,
in the mystery of sleep,
You ... restore, refresh, renew.

Recreate a right spirit within me, O God.   AMEN

Scripture Readings

> Psalm 116   *Return, O my soul, to your rest*
> Isaiah 30:15   *In rest you shall be saved*

Blessing

> May the gentle rhythm of your breath
> in the quietness of your heart
> keep on inviting you into
> the rest of God.   AMEN

Eternal

The water that I will give will become in them a spring of water gushing up to eternal life.

~ John 4:14 ~

Meditation

Some have seen Heaven in a wild flower;
others
have held the infinite in the palm of their hands,
experiencing eternity
as they exhale.

How can we ever know now
what it will look like in the age to come?

It curves beyond the horizon
of my imagination,
out of reach,
out of time.

Will it always flow beyond my knowing,
trickling through my fingers?
Sometimes it seems so distant.

Yet

here
now
within ...

Morning Prayer

As my eyes adjust to the morning light
and my vision begins to extend further,
reaching the familiar
wondering at the not yet,
Lord, help me to see the eternal
in all of life this day,
be present to the divine beauty in all creation,
recognise the caring Creator waiting to be invited in
to the height and depth of our day.

May we be carriers of the living water
that satiates all who are thirsty.   AMEN

Evening Prayer

When I walked with those who were thirsty,
did I give them Your water to drink?
When I found myself with an overflowing cup,
did I strive to capture what I did not need
or did I let it flow,
cascading into the dust?

As I lie down to rest,
quench my thirst again, O Lord,
that I may know Your eternal peace.

And if I am granted to wake once more,
may Your living water spring up in me
as we journey together
towards all that is eternal.   AMEN

Scripture Readings

John 4:14   *A spring of water gushing up
              to eternal life*
Mark 10:17   *'Good Teacher, what must I do
              to inherit eternal life?'*

Blessing

When waters rage,
God's peace.
When waters still,
God's awakening.
When water is scarce,
God's blessing.
When water flows,
God's grace.   AMEN

HOW WE PRAY

TWELVE ARTICLES ON PRAYING IN DIFFERENT CONTEXTS

Rejoice always, pray without ceasing,
give thanks in all circumstances; for this is
the will of God in Christ Jesus for you.

~ 1 Thessalonians 5:16–18 ~

Praying Prophetically

'Your kingdom come. Your will be done, on earth as it is in heaven.'

~ Matthew 6:10 ~

What would the world be like if Jesus' prayerful longing was fully, resoundingly satisfied?

Stop there. Seriously immerse yourself in this question. Be soaked in the dream of God for as long as you can bear it. Envisage, in all the depth you can, how the world might be if God's dreams were reality. People thriving and looking out for each other. Nature flourishing. Respect, safety, friendliness and fairness as givens. Societies fostering the wellbeing of all and serving the common good.

Be lost in the detail, whether global or local. Try writing it down. Imagine and describe one small corner of this new earth. Open your mind and heart to the yearning of God.

Praying prophetically is the response evoked from our longing-with-God for a world of more justice, more trust, more equality, more love. It is the response, too, that arises from lamenting the suffering we see and protesting its causes; from wrestling with how we can be faithful in Kingdom-building as we long to be free of inertia and despair; from questioning dehumanising systems and seeking God's wisdom on how to act.

I recently heard a young man, William, tell his life's story… his upbringing in Glasgow, struggling at school yet excelling at sport and singing, the peer pressure that pulled him into a street gang, his eventual estrangement from his family and subsequent frightening months of sleeping rough. Despite these desperate circumstances, he expected life to quickly turn out better. He spoke of finding a hostel place then eventually being allocated a two-bedroom flat as his first and cherished own home.

It was bigger than William needed but no smaller flats were available. He loved his flat, a place of safety and security from which to flourish at last. Then came the 'bedroom tax'. Unable to manage on the reduced housing benefit, William was evicted and found himself back in a hostel. Still, his life's motto, he said, was 'Never give up on yourself.'

Praying prophetically means grieving with God over stories like William's and never giving up – on him, ourselves, our prayers or our God.

And when we have no words of our own, our great allies the prophets have cried out before us. Where conflict has broken out, we yearn as Habakkuk did:

O Lord, how long shall I cry for help,
  and You will not listen? ...
Destruction and violence are before me;
  strife and contention arise.
So the law becomes slack
  and justice never prevails.

~ Habakkuk 1:2, 3–4 ~

With Jeremiah we still question the apparent success of those who behave destructively:

Why does the way of the guilty prosper?
  Why do all who are treacherous thrive?

~ Jeremiah 12:1 ~

And Amos passionately declared, as well we might, to those who practised greed and dishonesty:

Hear this, you that trample on the needy,
  and bring to ruin the poor of the land,
  saying, 'When will the new moon be over
  so that we may sell grain ...
and practise deceit with false balances,
buying the poor for silver
  and the needy for a pair of sandals...'
The Lord has sworn by the pride of Jacob: ...

I will turn your feasts into mourning,
  and all your songs into lamentation…

~ Amos 8:4, 5–6, 7, 10 ~

Joel painfully described how his people's land and food supplies were utterly devastated by swarms of locusts. His words might help us pray for those blighted by famine:

For a nation has invaded our land,
  powerful and innumerable…
It has laid waste my vines,
  and splintered my fig trees…

~ Joel 1:6, 7 ~

To the ensuing despair and physical hunger, Joel spoke encouragement to trust God's reassurance of restoration, again a cry to never give up:

I will pour out my Spirit on all people…

~ Joel 2:28 (NIV) ~

Speaking honestly and fearlessly to God and to the world is not for the fainthearted. Prophets then and now are pray-ers immersed in the currents and tides, dreams and visions of where they are. As we eat, sleep and breathe 2017 Scotland, what are we yearning for with God; what do we ask of God; what complaints will we throw at God; what perspectives will we offer to God's scrutiny; what will we seek God's courage and compassion to speak out about and act on?

Another worthwhile prayer exercise might be to write a prophetic-style oracle that captures and expresses some of your deepest cries to God and pleas to society. Begin with the situation as it is. Complain, protest, grieve and question. Then ask for help and dream of restoration. Never give up.

Written by JO LOVE

PRAYER NOTES

Praying in Difficult Circumstances

And He told them a parable to the effect that they ought always to pray and not lose heart.

~ Luke 18:1 (ESV) ~

Some circumstances are not only difficult but seem at first almost impossible. I once asked a hospital chaplain what he prayed when there was no hope of viable life for the patient he was with. He replied that he had noticed in John's Gospel, chapter 12, that Jesus, having looked at the grim destiny that awaited Him seemed to have a moment of crisis: *'Now is my soul troubled – what shall I say?'* In the end, however, He steadied himself by simply saying, *'Father, glorify Thy name.'*

'That made sense,' said the chaplain, 'so whenever I find myself at the bedside of someone who is alive but beyond apparent recovery, I simply pray: *"Father, glorify Your name – in this person's life."*'

That chaplain was right. When things are dark, we may not know what to say or do, but God does, so we acknowledge that and hand it to Him.

That 'handing over' takes us to our second point. Scripture tells us that Jesus took authority over whatever stood opposed to God's good will for us. He then handed that authority over to us. This means that when we are in a dark place and feel assailed by trial and trouble, we should not feel intimidated from taking command of the situation in His name.

We start with an affirmation, such as, *'Greater is He that is in me than he that is in the world.'* In Jesus' name we bind whatever bad force is thwarting God's benign will for us; then we order it to be gone, and finally we hand the situation over to God. Since we know He will take all of it on His shoulders, that means if thereafter we still have the stress of it, then we still haven't given it all to Him.

That brings us to a third point, which is to do with care in the language we use in prayer at difficult times. When Jesus spoke to situations, He did not use 'if' or 'maybe', but – as in the raising of Lazarus – *'Thank You Father, that You have heard me.'* Clearly, our prayers are going to be more effective when made from within an atmosphere of positive, trust-filled language. Since we walk by faith and not by sight, we take care to speak words of life over even the most crushing and hopeless of circumstances. What's more, we keep on doing so. As Churchill famously said in a speech in 1941, *'Never give in, never give in, never, never, never, never.'*

Fourth, when a hard situation is troubling us and we turn to our prayers, there's something we perhaps need to think about first, and that is that God rarely does anything for us to keep us as we are. If all we want is for something to go back to what it was, then we are forgetting that in everything He is God the Creator, and His engagements with us are almost always to move us on. If we pray and feel He is not hearing us, it may be because He knows that we are not ready to accept His involvement as a means of going on.

So a good starting point is always to affirm that whatever happens, we are prepared to accept His lead on the matter. If that is a step too far, then we pray for Him to work on our feelings, saying, *'I am willing to be willing!'*

Fifth, remember that the word of God is alive and active. So keep a Bible verse up your sleeve for the tough times. This means that if things are so bad that you just can't manage to pray, then you still have something to hold onto and repeat to yourself.

Useful verses are *'Stand firm and see the victory of the Lord'* (2 Chronicles 20:17) or *'my God will supply every need of yours according to His riches in glory in Christ Jesus'* (Philippians 4:19) or *'He has rescued us from the power of darkness and brought us safe into the kingdom of His dear Son'* (Colossians 1:13).

Lastly, if even a Bible verse is beyond you, remember if nothing else, you are precious, you are loved and you are known. Life may batter and cut you, but you are not lost, you are God's and you do not walk alone.

Written by LAURENCE WHITLEY

PRAYER NOTES

Praying Pastorally

The Lord is my shepherd, I shall not want.

~ Psalm 23:1 ~

I'm still learning to pray pastorally. There are times when praying for someone else is a spontaneous reaction, but I'm frustrated by the times my prayers for others are reluctant and rushed. I want to learn more. I will try to describe what I am learning.

I love the image of God as a shepherd who cares for the flock. This image of God makes me want to pray. It teaches me that praying pastorally is when sheep cry out to the shepherd because they are concerned for other sheep. It tells me that it is in God's nature to care for me and the people I am praying for.

I wanted to find out more about a shepherd's way of living. I read James Rebanks' best-selling book *The Shepherd's Life*, which ends with a description of a shepherd's instinct to care for the sheep:

> *When I leave my flock in the fells surrounded by grass and come down home, I leave something of myself with them ... sometimes I can't help myself, and go back up to the fell just to see all is well.*

~ James Rebanks, *The Shepherd's Life* ~

This shepherd's depth of care for his sheep amazed me. I wanted to keep learning more about the Lord who is my shepherd.

Isaiah's description of God as a shepherd draws me again and again. It leads me to trust that God is present with the people I'm praying for.

> *Like a shepherd, He will care for His flock,*
> *gathering the lambs in His arms,*
> *Hugging them as He carries them,*
> *leading the nursing ewes to good pasture.*

~ Isaiah 40:11 (*The Message Bible*) ~

Such vivid pastoral care makes me want to take time and picture this scene as I pray.

I picture a shepherd and a flock. I picture God and those I pray for. The shepherd is among the flock; God is among the people I pray for.

I picture the weather. It might be balmy or blowing a gale, but the shepherd is there. God is there in the operating theatre, there in the exam room, there in the job interview, there wherever the people I pray for are.

I picture the shepherd and the lambs. The shepherd has noticed the ones struggling to walk and is carrying them over rough and steep ground. God has noticed the people I pray for. God has noticed the one struggling with family, the one struggling with money. God is carrying them.

I picture the shepherd hugging the lambs. The shepherd feels the heartbeat of the lambs, and the lambs feel the heartbeat of the shepherd. I pray for the heartbeat of God's love to fill the people I am bringing to God.

I picture the shepherd leading the nursing ewes to good pasture. I ask God to lead those with family – adjusting to new babies, encouraging teenagers or caring for family who are getting frail.

I have tried to learn to look more closely at God the shepherd. But I also want to learn to pay more attention to the people I pray for. I need to do this. I know I hurry through praying from one person to the next. I know my prayers can lapse into giving God my advice about what the person I'm praying for should do next. I want to learn to pray more deeply for others.

I began to take more notice of how Paul began his pastoral letters. Near the start of each letter, Paul gave thanks to God for the people he was writing to. He gave thanks for the faithful and generous Philippians, he gave thanks for anxious Timothy, he gave thanks for the difficult Corinthians. I am trying to learn to always give thanks for the people I pray for. I am finding I take longer to pray for them. I am finding I enjoy thanking God for them. I am finding that I am more likely to bring them to God as they really are.

I have still got so much to learn about praying pastorally. There is my own laziness to overcome. There are questions for me to work through about the ways God answers prayer. But since God longs for us to pray and since God is the shepherd, God will keep teaching the flock to pray for each other.

Written by DANIEL CARMICHAEL

PRAYER NOTES

Praying with Disability

Come and enter my multi-sensory world,
a world where nothing is quite as you see ...
a magical world I'll show you,
full of surprises, come enter with me!

A world where forest green
    ... is the scent of a 100-foot fir tree;
where winter white
    ... is the wind when it bites through your clothes;
where cobalt blue
    ... is the warmth of a pool.
I can swish my legs and splash like a shining seal.
Look at me!
I am free!
I can swim like a shimmering fish in the sea!

I may be blind but can you see
gazing with my secret eye,
my world is very multi-sensory ...
What's your world like?

~ Katriona Goode ~

This poem was written about our disabled son, Matthew, when he was only about 7 years old. It was published in a book produced by the children's hospice Helen House in Oxford. Matthew has had a challenging life journey. Following five months in hospital when he was two years old, he was accepted for respite at the hospice. Prayers were an important focus throughout that time.

Matthew's name means 'God's gift' in Hebrew and that is exactly what he is to us every day of our lives. Now a young man of 19, he lives at home full time with care support. He is a member of our local church in the Scottish Borders and has affirmed his faith in God in a bespoke service themed 'I have the joy of the lord'.

Prayer has been hugely important in our lives as a family. We have prayed and prayed for healing, for miracles, for getting through the day and night, for Matthew's survival. Without God in our lives, I just don't know how we would have got through our journey together, for the road has been very rocky indeed.

Matthew's story is quite remarkable. He has severe disabilities: cerebral palsy affecting all four limbs, making co-ordination very difficult – any movement is hard for him to control. He uses a wheelchair and cannot walk. He is non-verbal but often very joyfully vocal, especially during the hymns in church! He is cortically blind and is fed by a gastric tube. He has complex needs. He loves music and has learned to control his voice, vocalising at the appropriate times within the service. Only by regular attendance and understanding the shape of the worship has he been able to develop this skill. He has always gone to church since he was a wee baby. We, his parents, have done everything in our power to help him develop whatever skills he can.

One very key skill is pressing a switch. Matthew has a communication aid called a BIG MAC (it looks a bit like a large red smarty). We record our voice onto the switch and then Matthew can press it to share his news. For he loves to communicate. We have used it so that he can say 'hallo' and introduce himself, to tell his news from home and school, or to join in with a phrase in a song or a story. It is a most simple and joyful piece of equipment. It has taken years to teach Matthew to use this switch consistently.

I have been writing prayers for our local church for some time now. When we decided we wanted to all worship there together as a family, it was because we wanted Matthew to become known in our village and to be an active member of our community. So it wasn't long before I came up with idea of him using this very switch as an integral part of the prayers. It has revolutionised our worship as a family and greatly enriched the church congregation. It has helped break down barriers in disability, and meant people now come forward naturally to speak with Matthew, as they have learnt how to communicate with him.

I specifically write the prayers with a response. Matthew has the key role to press at the right moment, leading the response of the prayers and triggering the congregation to follow him.

I also use sound as a way of prayerful expression, taking the multisensory approach and bringing the world of nature outside into the church itself. We use birdsong and small toys that reflect our local countryside: sheep bleating, cows mooing and birds tweeting, their sounds becoming a focus of thanks within the prayers. I have also made prayers in an Iona format, and I have even played seawash in the background once. My prayers are always very Celtic influenced, because of the wonderful Borders countryside – it is inspiring to see God around every day, as I look out onto the hills from our home.

Usually I take a theme from a reading or a hymn and include that within the prayers. Here is an example of some opening prayers we made together in June 2016:

> *Matthew is going to help with the opening prayers today.*

> *So when Matthew says:*
> **Lord as the sun and stars shine,**

> *The congregation responds:*
> ***May we shine with Your love.***

> *Lord, so often in our day-to-day lives,*
> *everything becomes very fast;*
> *we forget to take time to stand and stare,*
> *to be still.*
> *We don't find time to notice the beauty of Your world*
> *in the warmth of the early summer sun;*
> *in the bright white light of a moonlit night;*

in the glory of the millions of stars that pinprick the night sky;
in the moon and stars that guide our way through the darkness.

Lord as the sun and stars shine,
May we shine with Your love.

Lord we need to take time to be still and to know that You are God;
to feel Your Holy Spirit, around us every day and within us;
to feel Your presence now, as we gather together here in this church.

Lord as the sun and stars shine,
May we shine with Your love.

We thank You for this time to feel Your peace and calm upon us.
We thank You that we may worship and praise Your holy name in safety and peace without fear of persecution.

Lord as the sun and stars shine,
May we shine with Your love.

As we are gathered here together in this place, open our hearts to feel Your love;
open our ears to listen and hear Your word;
open our minds to understand what Your spirit is telling us.
Pour out Your spirit onto us all today, so that we may draw closer to You.

Lord as the sun and stars shine,
May we shine with Your love.

Disability is very challenging. It can be limiting, frustrating. It can close many doors. With Matthew's help, the church door has been opened to accept him.

He has learned to demonstrate his spirituality through prayer connecting to God's Holy Spirit with his joy. We thank God for that every day. This is how Matthew has taught us to pray.

Written by KATRIONA GOODE

PRAYER NOTES

Praying through Conflict

'Conflict opens a path,
a holy path,
towards revelation and reconciliation'

~ John Paul Lederach, *Reconcile:*
conflict transformation for ordinary Christians ~

In the midst of conflict, when we can feel caught up in despair, confusion and deep separation, we may, with the psalmists, turn to prayers of anguish and lament. Working and living through conflict can be tough. At the same time, in Place for Hope we affirm, with Lederach, that conflict can open up a path, a holy path towards inner and outer transformation. When conflict is transformed and relationships are healed, we may also offer prayers of thanks, gratitude and joy.

In prayer we turn humbly towards God; we ask for help; and we remain open to a response. When we find ourselves in a broken relationship, a divided community, a church at loggerheads, or overwhelmed by the violence in the world, the same three-fold prayer dynamic persists: turn to God, seek help, and remain open to the surprise of the Holy Spirit.

In prayer, turn to God

In turning to God in times of conflict we immediately acknowledge that we are not alone. No matter how wise we are as human beings, in prayer we acknowledge a deeper, wider mystery and faith. The very act of turning to God can itself be the start of a process of reconciliation: in turning, we turn inwards to the wisdom of God. This inner turning is also an invitation to consider, in humility, the part we ourselves may be playing in the conflict. In turning to God, we also turn outwards, opening ourselves to the possibility that new ways may be found to respond to conflict, difference and change – both in ourselves and in the other. Turning outwards, we may find ourselves turning to face the other – perhaps the one opposed – and so find ourselves on the path to transformation.

In turning to God we pray: *'In You, O Lord, I put my trust.'* And so we discover anew the wisdom of the Lord's prayer: *'Your kingdom come, Your will be done.'* In turning humbly to God we begin by asking: *'What is Your will, dear God?'*

In prayer, ask for help

The Psalms tell many stories of enemies, hatred, revenge killing and the abuse of power. These are stories with echoes for today. Yet Scripture, and the Psalms also reveal to us the persistence and faith of God's people who, in times of awful trouble, continue to turn to God in prayer for help. Psalm 46 sets the tone: *'God is our refuge and strength, a very present help in trouble.'*

This ever-present God is affirmed again in Matthew 18, when, in a chapter full of conflict, we read *'where two or three are gathered in My name, I am there among them'*, or in other words, *'when you are in trouble, and you ask for My help, know that I am already there among you.'* Events may not turn out as we wish, or expect – but we can be sure that when we ask for help in prayer, we, all of us seeking transformation, will receive it. We are not alone.

In prayer, remain open to the surprise of the Holy Spirit

Isaac and Rebekah, when their prayers for a child were answered, may have been surprised not only by the miracle of life, or by the awful conflict between their boys: they may have been equally surprised by the eventual reconciliation experienced. Jacob and Esau may have been destined to become sworn enemies but the story of their reconciliation gives us hope: the experience of humiliation by the other, of running away from our enemy, and then with God's help of finding the strength to turn towards and to greet the enemy are all present in this story (Genesis 25 ff.). As we remain open to the surprise of the Holy Spirit in prayer, we may discover that what seems to be an intractable and unbearable conflict carries with it deeper truths that can transform our lives and the lives of those around us.

In times of conflict ...

In times of conflict it can be helpful to:

- take time to be still
- turn to God in openness and humility
- seek the help of God, and of others around you to understand the differences that face you
- be prepared to be surprised by the gift of the Holy Spirit
- trust that conflict can 'open up a holy path' to transformation.

Written by RUTH HARVEY

Ruth Harvey is Director of Place for Hope,
www.placeforhope.org.uk

PRAYER NOTES

Praying with Scripture

Tradition is large. It is crammed with a wonderful range of pictures of God – as seamstress sewing clothes for Adam and Eve, as architect designing the ark and the temple, as a dinner party host, as wind, as fire and rock and water. We need such storehouses of images to elaborate our own views…

~ Ann and Barry Ulanov, *The Healing Imagination* ~

A bigger story meets our own

In a society of high stimulation, moving images and rapid change, how can we pray in a way that also brings colour, creativity, surprise *and* is an anchor in our lives?

I have found that 'imaginative prayer' opens doors to new experiences of myself and of God. When I think prayer 'should' be quiet and holy but my being yearns for a more obvious life-impacting connection, praying imaginatively with Scripture has brought something visceral or yet deeply intimate.

Let's take Jacob, for example (Genesis 32:22–32), locked in a battle with an angel? With God? With himself? I've prayed with this story many times when I've felt tossed about by life, wrestling with myself or others. I've found companionship with Jacob who 'wins' – in terms of keeping his life – but who is wounded. I have come through alive, but changed forever, and bearing the scars. And like Jacob I have been touched by God.

Blind Bartimaeus (Mark 10:46–52) calls on Jesus passing by and, in imagination, I have heard Jesus' same question to Bartimaeus echoing in my own life: *'What do you want me to do for you?'* Surely Bartimaeus' answer was obvious, with his unseeing eyes? But as I imagined this character from long ago,

I have discovered some unexpected responses of my own. What is it that I *really* want of God?

And Mary, oh Mary, the womanly ally and motherly friend I have come to know through imaginative prayer using various passages: a small cosy stone house, baking bread in the kitchen, Jesus popping in occasionally, a stone window seat and a carpenter's rocking chair, places I return to talk and find comfort 'when all else fails' (and why not sooner?). I know this place well.

Scripture is full of symbol and metaphor: Jesus' sermons, parables and life stories often bring unexpected images – a camel through the eye of a needle, pigs flinging themselves over a cliff, a bleeding woman. Imagination, like our senses, is a gift from God. Used reflectively with discernment, it leads us to insight and ongoing revelation of self and of God.

St Ignatius, in particular, encouraged the use of imagination in his 16th-century *Spiritual Exercises*, a series of prayerful and deepening meditations around the life of Christ. Rediscovered by today's spiritual seekers and pilgrims, you can 'Pray Now' using this same imaginative method in simple steps:

- Choose a passage – narrative stories from the Gospels are often a good place to begin.

- Find a comfortable yet attentive place and allow yourself to simply arrive. I often light a candle and take a couple of slower breaths, beginning to touch in to wherever I find myself on the inside *and* to the sense of 'the more than'.

- Take a few moments to consider what you hope for as you begin this prayer. Ask God for what you most desire in your heart: what is the gift you are seeking today?

- Read the passage several times until you are familiar with the story. Don't try to make anything happen, but just listen to the story as a content child might listen at bedtime.

- Then slowly allow the scene to arise within you, taking your time. What initial image comes to mind? What do you see? Is it hot or raining? What do you smell, touch, hear? Use all your senses to 'see' the story.

- Who is there? And begin to notice where *you* are in the story: one of the characters, or someone looking on. Which part of the story do you identify with or see yourself in? Let the story unfold, without consciously directing it. Don't worry if things surprise you, or if the story develops a little differently from what you expect; God can come to us in many ways.

- What happens next? Is Jesus there? What do you find yourself saying or doing? How are you feeling as you are part of all this? Stay with the story as long you want to, waiting as it evolves.

In my own praying, I sometimes find surprising things strike me, and sometimes not much at all. But in either case, often a shift comes as I close the imaginative prayer and speak with God about what has just happened – or not happened! The more honest I am with God, the freer I feel, and then a new awareness may come; I am met by God - and Jesus' story meets my own.

Written by ELIZABETH WHITE

Elizabeth White is a spiritual director, trainer and pastoral supervisor who also coordinates the 'Adventures in Faith' adult learning programme in the Diocese of Edinburgh.
www.reflectivespaces.org.uk

PRAYER NOTES

Praying through Silence

*Our greatest need is to be silent before this great God
... for the only language He hears is the silent language
of love.*

~ St John of the Cross ~

God is our Great Lover. Slipping into silence is to be at
one with the One. Sharing in the *shalom* of the Sacred,
there is prayer beyond praying with words. In silence,
we listen to the silence of the Holy. In the darkness of
the soul, thinly held by tender transcendence, we delve
into the depthless deep, the climax of spiritual intimacy.
Silence is the pinnacle of Christian worship; it is the
destination of our inner journey.

Silence is not a technique; instead, we are surrendering
ourselves to the Sacred. We are learning to sit in the
presence of the One who loved us from before we were
conceived; we are learning to be at peace with the
Presence, consumed by our mutual love. We are ready
for silence when words in prayer are no longer adequate:
they are empty of meaning or somehow get in the way.

When we first begin the journey into silence, it is easy to
be distracted by sounds around us or thoughts within.
This is normal, but persevere. Be gentle with yourself,
forgiving, loving and patient. In time, you will find
praying with silence to be restorative, a source of
spiritual communion, and the sacred space from which
the peace, compassion and forgiveness of God radiate
from the soul's centre into the whole of your life.

It can be difficult to maintain silence because, as we still
ourselves, we can become distracted, remembering
practical tasks we have to complete or conversations we
have had. More challenging still are thoughts from the
past that may rise to the surface: personal failures, losses
or hurts. However, slowly, steadily, it is possible to
sensitively face these troubles and, in time, step beyond

them. Each time we are distracted, calmly, faithfully return to the silence, to the Sacred at the very core of our being. We are present in the present moment.

St Augustine said of God, *'You are closer to me than I am to myself.'* In spiritual nakedness, we have nothing to say, nothing to offer except our vulnerability, our very soul. Praying with silence soaks us in the Sacred.

In silence, we move into darkness. We leave behind concepts of the Divine and centre ourselves in the Presence. In silent prayer, we rest in the emptiness we call God. Spiritual practice is about being present to the Presence. Through this we may gain a truer and deeper sense of our inherent worth. God is the canvas on which the Cosmos is painted, the Transcendent indelibly woven in and through the world of matter and consciousness. In silent prayer, we are held in being, cherished and embraced by Eternity; vastness unvoiced.

The mystics have described God as the luminous darkness or the still and unmoved darkness. We ready ourselves for silent prayer by seeking a place of quiet and seclusion. Be still and sit with your back straight. Through meditation, at a measured pace, be aware of your head, neck, shoulders, back, arms, hands, legs, feet and toes. Roll your shoulders if there is any tension lingering in your muscles. Bring your focus back to the centre of your being, to the soul, the seat of God's Spirit within you: you are a God-Bearer.

Be aware of your breathing: God breathes through your breathing. In your breath is the *ruach*, the breath of God, giving you life and sustaining you. Concentrate on your breathing; let it ease and slow down. Be aware that God fills the space where you sit: the room, the sanctuary or the hillside. Learn to sit for 5 minutes, then 10 minutes, then 15 minutes and so on. The more we surrender ourselves into the silence of God, the more we will want to remain there. Be aware that God fills the vessel of your soul with drops of compassion, filling you to overflowing.

To enter silence, it may be helpful to repeat the name of Jesus, slowly, inwardly, allowing Him to draw near, be present to you. Another sacred word which you may use is *Maranatha*, a four syllable Aramaic word meaning '*Come, Lord*'.

As your soul becomes stilled, you may let go of the word and prayerfully listen to the silence, aware of the Absolute, the Spirit whom Jesus called Father. Be still.

Written by SCOTT MCKENNA

PRAYER NOTES

Praying with Children and Young People

*'Let the little children come to me; do not stop them;
for it is to such as these that the Kingdom of God
belongs.'*

~ Mark 10:14 ~

When we approach praying with children and young
people, our default position is often simply to think of
getting them to sit still with their hands together and eyes
closed, whilst we say some words and they respond at
the end by saying *'Amen'*, whether or not they've
listened, understood or even agreed with the words said.
We may vary where and when we pray with them – at
home before meals and at bedtime, or at church in
Sunday School or uniformed organisations – but the
technique used is still often the same.

As they develop cognitively, we find it harder to pray in
this way with them as they become more able to voice
and show their disengagement and simply opt out.

There is a difference between 'saying prayers' and
'praying'. When we approach praying with children and
young people, it is important to recognise that
distinction. Prayer isn't simply about technique; it's
about responding to what is going on in our lives through
conversation and relationship with God. Through our
interactions with children we need to enable them to
come to understand this for themselves.

Children have an innate spirituality which they need help
in expressing and developing, but that also means they
have much to offer us, so the best starting point is
through viewing them as joint pilgrims on the journey,
rather than people who need things done for them.

Through encouraging regular patterns of prayer in the
morning/at bedtime, before meals, when going on
holiday, on special occasions such as birthdays and

changing schools, when big events happen in the world such as government elections or natural disasters, through the liturgical seasons such as Advent and Lent, we show in practical ways that God is interested in all aspects of our lives. Children are spontaneous and by encouraging spontaneity, we show that all life is part of being with God, sometimes in unexpected places and at unusual times!

Churches and parents can do a lot to model and develop a culture and rhythm of prayer as individuals and families, as well as together in corporate worship.

Children are particularly good at picking up and mirroring the behaviour of those around them, so having some simple questions to explore together can aid the feeling of journeying and praying together:

- What are you thankful for?
- What are you wondering about?
- What do you need?
- What are you sorry for?
- What does the world need?
- What do the people we know need?

In these instances it would be important for the adult to be involved in the prayer too. For example, at bedtime a parent might say *'Today, God, I'm thankful for cups of tea with my friends'* and then the child might say *'Today, God, I really enjoyed playing on the swings and am thankful for Amy playing with me'*.

Just as there are different learning styles, recent research has shown there are different spiritual styles (ways of engaging with God) too: through word, symbol, emotion and action. Everyone may find prayer more fulfilling and easier in some ways than others; some prefer quiet reflection while others like exuberance. For those with a preference for the:

- word style – try praying through Scripture, and in particular the Psalms
- symbol style – try giving them something to hold or look at to focus on, or going on a prayer walk
- emotion style – try praying using music or in big groups
- action style – try praying about world issues or praying with and for other people.

We need to enable children and young people to be themselves as they pray, encouraging them to be honest about their worries, struggles, questions and feelings and to take time to listen to God's still, small voice. As each child and young person is unique and has different life experiences, they need the opportunity to pray in ways that are appropriate to their development and experience of faith and to how they engage with God.

Being creative and trying many different approaches enables children to experience something of the creativity of God whilst empowering them to find their own way to engage with God.

Written by ISOBEL BOOTH-CLIBBORN
and SUZI FARRANT

PRAYER NOTES

Praying in the Spirit

Likewise the Spirit helps us in our weakness; for we do not know how to pray as we ought, but the very Spirit intercedes with sighs too deep for words.

~ Romans 8:26 ~

I was in my mid-twenties when I first felt *compelled* to pray. At that time I was obsessed with climbing. It was early January and I was clinging to a frozen waterfall. Daylight was fading, my strength was failing, and on the final vertical sweep of ice, I became as frozen as the icy cascade itself. Exhausted, petrified, contemplating the horrific consequences of the bone-shattering plunge that now seemed inevitable, I began to pray. As I cried out to God for help, as I implored him to guide each swing of my ice axes, I picked and kicked my way up that final wall with flawless precision and assertive strength that I knew were beyond my own capacities to marshal.

But how does that unique and personal incident relate to 'praying in the Spirit'? For many, the phrase 'praying in the Spirit' evokes imaginings of experiences reserved for the most pious and earnest of saints – a state of being attainable only through hours of intense application and focused exertion. However, the wonderful and releasing truth is that God, in the person of the Holy Spirit, longs to motivate, inspire and guide us in prayer.

Prayer is not just a discipline, an exercise intended for strengthening spiritual muscle. It is first and foremost a gift of grace, an undeserved and sometimes unrequested gift of communication. When words will not come, when we have no idea how to pray, when we feel unable to muster God-ward thoughts, the Spirit 'intercedes', intervenes on our behalf, becomes our intermediary, and does that which we are unable to do.

While some have understood 'praying in the Spirit' as referring to the language used (i.e. a special prayer language or 'praying in tongues'), it also includes all prayer arising from the Spirit's presence and assistance. The Holy Spirit is, after all, our 'helper' or 'advocate', the One sent to teach us (John 14:26). It is the Spirit who stirs within us the desire to pray and encourages us to pray in certain ways. When we are tongue-tied or when adequate language eludes us, the Helper prays on our behalf.

While my experience on the frozen waterfall was of God's gracious intervention despite my lack of faith, it is clear from Paul's letters that 'prayer in the Spirit' is something to be consciously chosen and carefully cultivated. Indeed, it is to become so integral to our experience that we pray in the Spirit *'at all times'* and *'in every prayer and supplication'* (Ephesians 6:18).

Now that is quite a state of affairs to aspire to: that all our prayers are prompted and animated by the Spirit. But Paul is never one to dilute the demands of Christian apprenticeship. Neither, however, is he in the habit of leading believers into discouragement by suggesting that Spirit-inspired prayer can be conjured up by individual effort. Rather, Paul encourages all to aspire to a more 'authentic' (i.e. of undisputed origin, genuine) experience of prayer by being awake to the Spirit's ever-willing-to-help presence. Having urged his readers to *'Pray in the Spirit at all times'*, he spells out the practical means: *'To that end keep alert'* (Ephesians 6:18).

Being alert begins with being awake to God's presence: *'The Lord is near to all who call on Him'* (Psalm 145:18). It is one thing to accept God's omnipresence, another to allow it to transform our lives moment by moment. When we recognise that *'In Him we live and move and have our being'* (Acts 17:28), we realise that the presence of God's Spirit is the most fundamental and important aspect of every moment. That recognition transforms the here and now from mundane moment into 'holy ground'. To be alert is to be conscious of God's presence, to welcome it, to be open to the Spirit's working, deliberately unguarded.

For many people, acts of praise, worship and adoration are powerful means of fostering this awareness. The acrostic ACTS (Adoration, Confession, Thanksgiving and Supplication) is useful in saving our praying from descent into a mere recitation of wish lists. Some of us are especially aware of God's presence when immersed in nature; others are prompted most readily by cerebral reflection or in confronting the needs of others or in a host of other ways. We are each different and the Lord speaks to us in our mother tongue, guiding, inspiring and encouraging us in ways that only our Creator knows are most helpful for us. Knowing us perfectly, longing for genuine and honest communication, we can be assured that our Helper delights to lead us into 'praying in the Spirit'.

Written by STEVE AISTHORPE

PRAYER NOTES

Praying with Doubt

'My God, my God, why have You forsaken me?'
~ Psalm 22:1 ~

The first law of prayer is, do not lie to God.
~ Martin Luther ~

I'm grateful that the Gospels record the desperate cry of the distraught father *'Lord, I believe, help thou mine unbelief'* (Mark 9:24, AV). It's something we've all said: *'Lord I do believe, but I have my doubts, I'm not as sure as I'd like to be. I've still got lots of questions.'*

In these circumstances, I consider, 'Either this world is an accident, or it's not.' and I choose to believe it's not an accident. There *is* a Creator; there *is* a God.

After the Second World War, scratched on a dungeon wall in Cologne, were found these words:

I believe in the sun, even when I see it not.
I believe in love, even when I feel it not.
I believe in God, even when He is silent.

Then I remember Jesus – and that no one doubts He lived, and has changed the world forever.

Faith is not a mathematical equation with a proof; it's a gift and it's a choice. Our faith can be strong: when we feel as if we're on a mountain top, we see things clearly, we're elated and we'd like the feeling to last forever. But we have to go back down into the valley, where children are suffering, friends let us down and we face opposition; where our faith is tested and challenged; where doubts surface.

Faith always has a shadow side. That is not to say that there will continually be doubt, but it can happen, and we have to hold on and live through it, letting it teach us and transform us: to trust even more, to discover new depths, to be led to a different form of service or to a closer walk with God. As Richard Rohr explains, faith is having the security to live with the insecurity.

It's an inner stance, not just subscribing to certain credal statements, but having an attitude of trust in life itself, and in the Spirit behind the universe. It's believing in love, and it's living not by my egotism, or my fears or my judging, but with gratitude, humility and compassion.

When my faith is assailed by doubt, there are a number of practical things I do.

I seek the company of someone whose faith is stronger than mine. I join with believers in worship, even if I feel as if I am only there in body.

I allow music to restore my soul – or the hills, or the sea, or the sky, remembering that 'Creation is God's first Bible'.

I analyse where the doubts might be coming from. Is it tiredness? Disappointment? Loss? Loneliness? Have I done something wrong? Have I distanced myself from God? Do I need to be more honest with myself – and with God?

I read a passage from Scripture, perhaps from the Psalms (e.g. 22:1-2; 77:1-10; 130), where the writer pours his heart out, in his distress, his anger, his fears, and his doubts … and I remind myself that it's all right to have doubts. Even Paul acknowledges them:

> *We are afflicted in every way, but not crushed;*
> *perplexed, but not driven to despair*
>
> ~ 2 Corinthians 4:8 ~

I repeat Biblical texts, sing lines from hymns, or use prayers learned by heart:

> *O Christ the Master Carpenter,*
> *who at the last, through wood and nails,*
> *purchased our whole salvation,*

wield well Your tools in the workshop of Your world,
so that we, who come rough-hewn to Your bench,
may here be fashioned to a truer beauty of Your hand.
We ask it for Your own name's sake. Amen

I pray, with my doubt, *'Lord I believe, help thou mine unbelief.'* I close my eyes and picture Jesus, if I can, and I speak into the void, trying to be completely open, and to express just how I feel, as though Christ is standing in front of me.

Come bring your burdens to God, for Jesus will never say no.

I sit in silence. I give God 'Sabbath' time, even if it seems empty, or fruitless, or time wasted. I wait. I listen. I wait. I listen …

There will always be some doubt. If we attempt to deny it, we become fanatical and lacking in grace. If giants of the faith doubted, then I can live with doubt too – and live through it.

There will always be a place for wonder and awe and mystery. We don't know everything, but we do know enough, to live by faith, and hope, and love.

And enough to persevere in prayer.

Written by DAVID LUNAN

PRAYER NOTES

Praying for Healing

And ought not this woman, a daughter of Abraham
whom Satan bound for eighteen long years, be set free
from this bondage on the sabbath day?

~ Luke 13:16 ~

Praying for healing is not straightforward. People of
Jesus' time understood and explained illness in a way
that can appear foreign to us. Many of our scientific
ideas, and history of poor practice in healing ministry,
can prevent our engagement with this kind of prayer.
In addition, most of us have been taught to notice the
physical healing that Jesus offers, and yet within most of
these stories there are multiple layers of healing. The
short text from Luke above indicates that, for Jesus, this
healing involved several components:

- affirmation, calling her a daughter of Abraham,
  granting her equality with men
- reassurance that neither she nor her family were
  personally responsible for her ill health, by
  explaining in the terms of the culture of the time
  that Satan had bound her
- freedom from restrictive social and religious legalism
  that said that such healing could not be done on the
  Sabbath

... and so health is brought by challenging the law-
makers. Her status in the community is restored, and
through her physical healing she has purpose again and
is enabled to play a useful role.

These features accord well with some recognised current
healthcare policies here in Scotland. First, that poverty is
a major block to health. Second, that finding purpose and
a role in a community is a significant component for
health. The work of many churches to provide social
care that offers companionship, meaning and focus for

many isolated people is part of the continuing healing tradition of the gospel, as much as integrating the kind of prayer practices described below.

Connecting

There is a great comfort in knowing someone else is praying for you. Offer to pray for someone daily, at the same time, for a period like a week or a month. You can invite them to join in, tuning in with you and with God.

Healing Light

Imagine God's healing light in whatever part of the body is injured, and picture the body well and full of life. And/or light a candle and concentrate on the flame. Let its light speak to you of the healing light of God that surrounds and is within us all.

Sharing closeness of God

Sometimes when we pray, all the possible negative outcomes of the situation come tumbling through our minds. In order to keep your mind focused on the beauty and wonder of God, try remembering a moment when you experienced God close to you – a particular moment in a church, a favourite place, a sunrise or sunset. Remember – and then imagine the person you are praying for and bring them into this remembrance of the wonder of God's love.

Using our hands

We all know that a gentle touch of a hand at the right moment can bring the reality of love close. You can do this for yourself.

Place your hands over the parts of your body that are suffering and concentrate on God's love, or repeat a Bible verse to yourself. If it seems appropriate to do this for another person, check with them that they are happy for you to put a hand on them and make sure by keeping your eyes open initially, to see if they are truly relaxed with your hands on them.

Music

Music can bring healing; prayer can be singing. Sing a song for the person for whom you are praying, either with them or as you remember them. For yourself, work out what music you experience as prayerful and set aside time to let the music speak to you of the ever-present reality of God's healing love.

Praying with others

There may be occasions when one or two of you from your church are invited to visit someone who is ill. You can use any of the above suggestions. A vital ingredient in most healing is relaxation and calm for all involved, while keeping your heart and mind focused on God. Prepare by asking yourselves what will help you to create a 'healing space' where the love of God can surround you all with peace.

Another way of praying in twos or threes is for two of you to pray silently for the third person – listening, waiting upon God for a few minutes without words. Any of you may find coming into your mind a text, a word, a picture, like a message from God. Offer the 'message' without any interpretation. Through this, God can open doors, sometimes even to old hurts and painful memories. As you speak and pray about them, commit the situation into God's hands. There can be much release, forgiveness and healing. Take turns to pray for one another and be prepared to be surprised by God.

Written by JENNY WILLIAMS

Author of *Why Health Matters for Ministry*
(available online; type these terms into a search engine
'Church of Scotland Why Health Matters')

PRAYER NOTES

Praying through Art

The first demand any work of art makes upon us is surrender. Look. Listen. Receive. Get yourself out of the way.

~ C.S.Lewis, *An Experiment in Criticism* ~

A work of art is where the artist and the viewer meet. Visual artists spend years learning to notice and respond creatively to what everyone else has overlooked or ignored. Their creative response enables us to become more aware of the world around us and the realities of the human condition. Therefore, when we look at any work of art and we do so as patiently and attentively as we would when we meet a person, we open ourselves to new perspectives and insights. Doing so can introduce us to a way of praying, of responding to what we have seen by lifting our minds and our hearts to God. I think of this way of praying as having four movements: looking, listening, praying and waiting.

The first movement is looking. Take time to look slowly at the art work. Look at what it is made of, its shape and colours, the patterns it makes and its subject. Read it from top to bottom and let your eye wander across it, directed by the way the piece flows. Notice details and things that seem to be absent, where it is sited and what is around it. Does it have a title? Do this slowly and trust that the Holy Spirit is with you in the looking, giving you eyes to see.

The second movement is listening. Look again at the work. What of it do you remember when you close your eyes? What has the work said to you? Is there an idea that sparked in you while you were looking. Think about how you respond to the work, has it delighted you, resonated with you or challenged you in some way? You may find yourself thinking about something that seems detached from what you have been looking at, or focusing on just one element of the work. Give yourself time, trust that the Holy Spirit is within you, giving you ears to hear.

The third movement is praying. Tell God about how you have responded to the work, what it has made you feel and what you have been thinking. Let your prayer be conversational, trusting the Holy Spirit will give you the words to say as you pray.

The fourth movement is waiting. Wait quietly with God; trust that the God who loves you wants to spend time with you. You may feel you are doing nothing, but this is the most important of the four movements. Trust that the Holy Spirit is at work in the depths of your spirit, deepening your faith. Let the work and its message move from your head to your heart, to dwell there in silence.

Sent (shown in the photos below and overleaf) was an art installation made for Advent a few years ago.

You are invited to use the images of *Sent* in these pages as a example of the four movements of prayer.

- *Looking* – *Sent* was made from used envelopes that were arranged and hung between two pillars in the Renfield St Stephen's Church. They were in the shape of two enormous wings that dominated the space. The light caught them in interesting ways – the envelopes looked a bit like feathers of different colours and tone. Up close you could read the handwriting, examine the stamps and notice the subtle variations in the design of envelopes.

- *Listening* – The envelopes were the means by which messages had been sent. They were the wrappings around messages, containing letters and cards, which, at Christmas, might have said, 'with love from ...' They were like the angels carrying the message that God is come among us, that God is with us. At the time I made *Sent,* I was going through a family bereavement and in a gentle way the envelopes resonated with my grief as I thought about Christmas cards that had been sent and received or would no longer be exchanged. At the time, they reminded me that God was with me and other folk were alongside me.

- *Praying* – How have these images of *Sent* resonated with you? Share it with God in prayer.

- *Waiting* – When I was finding it hard to put it all into words, I found that waiting with *Sent* was a way of praying without words. Look again at the image and let all that you have received settle into your heart.

Written by PETER GARDNER

PRAYER NOTES

Acknowledgements

The 52 chapters of *Pray Now* 'Word of Life' were
written by: Fyfe Blair, Derek Browning, James Cathcart,
Adam Dillon, Roddy Hamilton, Ruth Harvey,
Tina Kemp, Jo Love, David Lunan, Andrew McGowan,
Scott McKenna, Scott McRoberts, Phill Mellstrom,
Angus Morrison, MaryAnn Rennie, Jock Stein,
Lezley Stewart, Terry Taylor, Jenny Williams and
Wendy Young.

Daily headline Scripture quotations are taken from the
New Revised Standard Version, © 1989 Division of
Christian Education of the National Council of Churches
of Christ in the United States of America, published by
Oxford University Press.

With special thanks to Phill Mellstrom, Lynn Hall and
Hugh Hillyard-Parker for their work in preparing the
final manuscript.